A Transformation of Humanity

*

From

Good *vs* Evil

To

Living in the Light

*

By **Arleen Lorrance**

(Originator of "Be the Change" 1970)

LP Publications • Scottsdale, AZ

Published by LP Publications

12000 N 90th Street #2025

Scottsdale, AZ 85260

The Teleos Institute World Wide Web site address is

https://www.teleosinstitute.com

First Edition, 2024

Printed in the United States of America

Contents

Dedicated

to the

Light Bearers

who live in

Unconditional Love

The Love Principles

Originated by ***Arleen Lorrance****, 1970*

Be the Change You Want to See happen rather than trying to change anyone else

Have No Expectations but Abundant Expectancy

Problems Are Opportunities

Provide Others with Opportunities to Give

Create Your Own Reality Consciously

Receive All People as Beautiful Exactly As They Are

Remember:

Choice is the Life Process

Be the Change

that is Coming

Introduction

Transformation is on the horizon.

I am ready. I hope you are too. I am ready for the next evolutionary step for human-kind. It is a major shift waiting to become a reality. For that to happen, I, as an individual, must make the crossing into the new. And then, as has always happened in the history of human beings, others will also make the crossing until the tipping point occurs and the "new" becomes the norm. This is why I hope you are ready too.

This kind of shifting has occurred many times in human history. We used to be bent over and hairy like the apes. Over eons we shed our "coats," and we learned to stand erect. Early on we focused on survival. Then we moved to thriving.

Today we live in a state of polarities where the prominent focus is good *vs* evil. This focus has been in place for thousands of years. The time has come to shift from good *vs* evil to *living in the Light.* We have been spinning our wheels long enough. The time is coming to let the old emphasis go. When that occurs, we will become our greater potential. I am ready to do this. To take the step that leads to the new paradigm shift for the whole human race. Are you ready?

A Major Shift

What is coming is so different, it is nothing short of miraculous. The change will come because the frequency band of the planet itself is changing. It is rising to the level of new alignment with the universe itself.

The transformation of humanity may not be instantaneous but it will be an accelerated evolutionary process because of the changing frequency relationship between the earth and the universe. The influence on humanity will be intense as the vibrational shift occurs.

Goodness and creativity will merge and form an atmosphere in which only what is in accord with the new vibration will be welcomed. If we listen, we can hear it occurring in the higher tones of the music of the spheres. The swirl of sound and light is escalating.

Humanity will shift from a focus on good *vs* evil to living in the Light! The transition will be from old, patterned ways of living to the realization of unlimited potential.

Our level of consciousness will reach new heights. Our lives will be illumined by the infusion of energy from finer frequencies we have never before experienced. Our beings will be lifted so that we respond only to the highest good available to us at any moment.

When humanity does this collectively, when we commit to expressions of greatness, our whole way of living will rise toward the frequency of the Divine. It is thrilling to know that we will take our place as co-creators. Anyone/anything that is lesser, that clings to who we used to be, will flounder and be unable to continue in the light of the new reality. They will have to adapt and evolve.

The transformation is coming ready or not, and it brings hope for humanity.

This vision I see is in accord with wisdom I have learned and practiced over the last 55 years. I have had glimpses of this transformation as well as experiences which have validated the glimpses. The future I see is good; it is beyond good. It is filled with wonder and achievement. I am excited to share this vision of the future with you so that we may all prepare for the future. Together we will become the new, the more.

What does it mean to transition from good to great?

Following the transformation, polarities of a new order will come into existence. Until now the polarities have been in the realm of positive *vs* negative, good *vs* evil, love *vs* hate, elation *vs* depression. A new measure will come into being. Every human expression will shift into the positive as a baseline from which to draw comparison. The polarity we encounter will be the elevation of that positive rather than what we have now, a negative to be overcome. We will, for example, shift from capable to confident, from affirming to optimistic, from stable to progressive, from pleased to ecstatic.

This new way of defining polarities will lift humanity to the next level of its evolution. "Happy" will never be enough when its polarity is "Joy-filled." "Learned" will be contrasted with "Brilliant." The new measure will take us to a realm of existence completely different from the one we currently create.

We are already on the verge of this even though we can't quite see it. But it is inherent in our makeup and ready to emerge.

Even with all the conflicts and contrary points of view, opinions, and arguments that dominate our world today, there is a basic feature that humans bring to the fore. People are "good."

We want the best for ourselves. We even want the best for others. Some of us want the best for everyone! If we see someone in trouble, we instinctively jump into action to help. This is because we are inherently good. We care, we are compassionate, we come together in times of collective crisis. We are forgiving, most of the time. We are still learning about unconditional love, but we do love. That we know *how* to love says that we can ready ourselves for a transformation in which we move from good to great.

A *great* human race will be entirely different from the one that walks the earth today. There will be profound changes in the way we live. We will shift from competition to cooperation, from judgment to receptivity and love.

One of the major changes will be our realization that we are equally a vital part of one large whole and that we are not separate from each other or from the planet on which we live.

Humanity is on the brink of this transformation. Paradoxically, it comes precisely *because* we have brought ourselves to the peak of divisiveness. Our troubles, our cantankerous interactions, our intransigence, have rendered us incapable of continuing in the stalemate. We have been stuck, refusing to listen to one another and we have begun to stagnate. It is as if we are dying in place as we hold fast to our *manufactured* convictions.

In nature when something dies, it is replaced by something new. A birthing always occurs. A new shoot on a dormant branch. Thus, it will be with humans. We cannot continue in our current mode, and this is a clear sign that our old ways of being are breaking apart so that we can open to a new mode of living.

Standing on the verge of collapse is exciting; we are approaching the lighted unknown and as the old crumbles, we cascade into a Holy New Reality.

The Tower card in the Tarot deck (see next page) depicts the collapse. It is not to be feared but to be welcomed. It tells us that what separates us is falling away. The voices of division will be silenced. We will embrace what is good and we will be infused with the potential for greatness.

We will stand in the new in amazement, in wonder. We will feel as if we have been reborn into a next level of being human. We will feel this because it will be true, it will have occurred. We will look around and discover that we are One. We are One Being.

From SEPARATION To ONENESS

I had the privilege of "awakening" and touching the finer frequency world and the Light. In 1969, I looked into the heart of a flower and watched the shape and substance of it be replaced by its essence, by its energy. I entered that energy and merged with it. In that experience my consciousness was completely altered. I became one with all that is. I came to know there is only One.

I could feel myself being filled with joy such as I had never known. I shifted into radiance. This has never diminished. It resides as a backdrop in my consciousness even as I dip back into the complexity of living in this world of matter.

I know that there is only One Self and that each of us is a unique participating cell in that One Self. This is unity.

The life we live today exists on the level of polarities rather than unity. There is darkness and there is light. There is this side of an issue or that. Oddly, our very differences, the sides we take, keep everything in balance, albeit with difficulty and aggravation. We have lived in a world of good versus evil. Oneness exists just beyond this dichotomy.

When humankind comes to know this, to experience it, then conflict, contrary behavior, arguments, taking sides, and starting wars will fall away. From our current viewpoint it is impossible to envision such a major shift.

In our world of polarities, we think we are "right," and we think we can vanquish those who do things differently or hold different beliefs. The time is coming to give that up. None of it works. It has never worked. We have wars. We have peace. We have wars again. It's us *vs* them. It's good *vs* evil. It's the perpetual spinning that leads to nothing more, nothing new.

Why do we live this way? Because many of us live under the illusion that we are separate from one another. Big mistake. If we create this illusion, it is always "us" *vs* "them."

In the coming transformation we will know that we are One. Knowing that we are One Being, that we are cells in the One Being, we can embrace the whole and rejoice that we are in it and part of it. There is no point to attacking someone else because, as cells in the One Body, we are then really attacking ourselves! That is bizarre. Going to war with others is going to war with self. Killing others is killing self. It is time to move on and that time is coming.

Trying to Fix Things

In the meantime, in this stage before transformation, we try to remedy the problems we face. Because we are "good" people, we try to fix things. When we do that, we enter the problem, seek to move its heavy load, and to bring about change. But in the end, we are usually just moving the situation from one position to another. We are in and of the problem trying to change it. Worse still, what we often try to do is change the other side. Trying to change others is a useless endeavor, but it is a natural modality while living as if in separation and in polarities of positive vs negative.

We don't yet see that we need to lift above all of it. Not get involved or embroiled. We need to create a new reality and start from a place that embraces the whole. This will lead us from good to great, to living in the Light. This is what is coming in the transformation.

Before I had my awakening, I had no idea about Oneness. I lived my life as if I were separate from everyone and I valued being an individual. Like most people, I gravitated toward groups of like-minded people or those with whom I shared interests. This gave me a sense of belonging. Most of us have this to one degree or another. We have loving families where we belong. We have organizations where we are members. We have groups of friends. We have religious communities where we worship together and many beliefs we share with others.

Each of these connections represents the simplest level of uniting with one another. It is a form of sharing who we are. We contribute to one another. Because we have each other, we lift each other up and we are better for what we bring to each other. Each of us serves as a balancing force for what is missing in the other. All of this represents the best of who we are right now. We are there for each other.

We Are Each Other

The next step for humanity is to know that we are each other. There is no separation. We are all, each one, a single cell in One Manifested Being.

I never knew this before I looked into that flower, entered the energy world, and merged with all that is. That experience said, God is not something separate from us. It opened me to see that I/we are expressions of God in materialization. We are cells in the body of God so that the Creative Force can see itself in form.

We are each other. I had an experience of this with another human being recently. We met walking down the hall of our residence. I was on my way to the pool. She said, "I get cold just thinking of going swimming." She held out her hands and said, "See how blue my hands are. I have such poor circulation."

The moment she said that I lifted within myself to merge with her. I took her hands in mine and rubbed them to bring warmth and encourage circulation. She immediately responded by letting her hands melt into mine. It was as if there was no separation between the four hands. In truth, there was no separation (other than what exists in our minds where I think I am I and she thinks she is she.)

Next, I put my hands above hers and began to move the energy. She had never experienced this before but opened to it immediately. "I can feel that." she said. "That is wonderful." We became one energy field and color began to come into her hands (our hands.) When we finished and parted, she said, "I won't ever forget that, and I will do that for myself. I will move the energy." As I continued down the hall, I felt the "other" half of myself walking in the other direction toward her apartment.

I have experiences such as this many times a day. I see it as a beginning toward all of us knowing ourselves as One. I bring up Light in myself and radiate it through a warm smile. I watch as others coming toward me light up in the flow and emit their own radiance. We are practicing our awareness of Oneness. If God were looking at Itself in manifestation in those moments, It would see Its cells moving in and out of one another, in Light, in Oneness.

There are so many examples of this on the planet every day. Every time one of us sees the face of a newborn or a baby or a tiny child, we change. Our expression shifts. We become one with the miracle of life right before us. We cannot stop the smile that crosses our face; it comes organically because we automatically marvel at creation. We become One.

Oneness in Diversity

There are other examples of the experience of Oneness, some of which manifest as severe illnesses, such as PTSD. I watched a former soldier describe his agony over having participated in war. He wept because he had killed. He needed extensive counseling to cope with his actions even though it was "the enemy" he had slain. He might not have used these words, but he suffered because he was One with the man he had killed.

War is the antithesis of the creative process. It is the destruction of human life in the service of ideas and causes. Military people are trained to triumph, to kill, all in the name of saving their side. Yet, when they are on the field of battle, the enemy they see is a human being. They are asked to take a life. Most never talk about it later. They swallow what they did or find a way to justify their action. But if they allow themselves to feel, they confront destruction, and it is devastating. And if we extend their experience to Oneness, he who has killed has killed self, has killed a cell in the body of the whole.

We can go on having wars and conflicts only as long as we think we are separate. We have been "separate" for eons. Embroiled in we vs they. With the transformation we will move beyond that way of being. We will know we are each other.

As I explored the heart of the vision of the transformation that is coming, I wondered, when everyone realizes we are one being will we all hold the same view of everything? It was hard for me to imagine that because if we did there would be no need for many of us; one of us would suffice.

Then how will we know ourselves as one cell in the body of the whole if we have different points of view, if we take different sides of issues? I saw that we will do it by welcoming and acknowledging all sides equally. We will move from taking sides to laying our differences side-by-side, each having equal weight and value.

As we explore issues large and small, we will share one over-arching purpose: to lift all our life expressions so that they benefit the whole world. This will turn all problems into wonderful opportunities to enrich human life, indeed, to enrich all living things. Each of us will be challenged to resolve our differences by including everyone and every point of view. Everyone will seek to nurture, to bless, to unite so that we arrive at answers that move us from good to great.

I am excited to see that humans will reach such a harmonious level and I look forward to that shift. We will honor each other by doing what is appropriate for each of us, refraining from seeking to impose that on others, and focusing our entire attention on what will benefit the whole.

Living Together in Harmony

Each cell in the body of the whole will live out its mission and simultaneously honor the other cells in the body by receiving the choices they make without judging them. Cells living together in harmony make up the One and make room for all possibilities.

One size does not fit all, one position is not true for everyone. We all have points of view and choices to make. Trying to force others to live by our point of view further separates us. Labeling one position as good and the other as evil divides us.

If there are two or more ways to approach an issue and we have choices to make, it is because there are two or more approaches. If there were one way only, that is what would be available to us. There would be no discussion.

Over time, in human life, we have gradually come to singular places, one point of view that we agreed upon and we lived together in that union. For example, around the entire world we have become one in our mutual regard for traffic lights and stop signs. We came to this agreement for the benefit of the whole. It is our mutual decision. It is our way of reverencing life. We see and know what can happen when someone breaks this universal agreement. It is something of a holy moment, if we think about it, that all over the world people stop and wait until it is their turn. I see this as an achievement of greatness. Oneness in action, mutual caring for each other.

The point is, we arrived at traffic control together for the good of everyone. We moved beyond polarities and focused together on a basic need. Hence, today, we have a reoccurring miracle throughout the day where life is valued as precious.

We arrived at this juncture by seeing that we had an opportunity to live together. We shifted to function as one being.

Overcoming Division

In our current world of polarities, there are issues where we cannot "live and let live" unless we acknowledge that we are One Being, single cells in the body of the whole. We divide ourselves, take intransigent positions, and create a climate which is not healthy for anyone. There are many examples of this.

Heterosexuals who are very conservative religiously and politically, are uncomfortable with or opposed to equal rights and status for members of the LGBTQ+ and Trans community. "Straight" folks often cannot even conceive of two same sex people "making love." It rarely occurs to them that the same might be true on the other side of the issue. Namely, how can anyone want to have sex with a different sex? I was once told this by a gay man. He simply could not fathom engaging physically with a woman.

And now that the issue of Trans looms large and individuals are coming forth to proclaim they are in the wrong body, many in the "straight" world throw their hands up in the air, not being able to comprehend.

This situation provides us with great opportunities to practice honoring and receiving everyone as they see themselves. How do we do this? When the coming transformation occurs, we will want to. We shall open and make room for all expressions of human beings whether we understand them or not. We shall cease making them "the other." We will know that they too are cells in the body of the One. We will make room for each other because we will know that to do anything else denies the viability of the life of the whole.

In the coming transformation I envision that people will walk down the street and celebrate every kind of coupling they see, every kind of expression of self, sexually and otherwise. Look, he and she are holding hands. Clearly, they love each other. Look, here comes a tall being who was once a man and is now an elegant woman. Walking down the street and marveling at the variety. Seeing how many different expressions of human beings there can be. Knowing that each is an equal cell in the body of the whole. We will go a step further to acknowledge that this is what God, The Creative Force, is seeing of Itself on the street of life.

Another issue where we currently divide ourselves in our world of positive and negative polarities is in relation to religious beliefs and how they differ. There are those who believe in multiple Gods. On a trip to Nepal, we learned there are thousands of Gods each having a different responsibility. In India, God is divided into different expressions and these rule over the various aspects of life. Christians and Jews have One God; one has a savior, Jesus, the other is still waiting for one to appear. Muslims also adhere to monotheism. They refer to the unity of God as Allah and rely on Muhammad as his messenger. Buddhism is called a non-theistic faith where no god is worshipped. It is more a philosophy or moral code which focuses on the causes of suffering. There are other beliefs and designations.

We divide ourselves into these different religions and beliefs. Unfortunately, that often separates us rather than unites us when we struggle over who has the best approach to Truth.

There are agnostics who aren't sure about what is true and non-believers who chuck all of it and steer clear of belief systems.

A basic quality of humans is that we are "good." Sometimes we slip and do or say things that are less than good and require that we make an adjustment. Religion can be said to be a way of reinforcing goodness. It helps us to keep ourselves in check and when we commit acts that are deemed immoral, we have outlets to seek forgiveness and to help change our behavior.

Some people have no concept of needing redemption. They don't believe in heaven or hell. They weren't born in sin, so they have no need for redemption. They won't go to hell because they don't believe in it, nor will they go to heaven because they don't believe in that either.

We deal with all of this by honoring our

own beliefs and even though this represents separation, we mostly make room for each other and find ways to get along. Problems arise when any one group tries to dominate the others by imposing their beliefs on public school systems, on legislation and the like. In the United States we have separation of church and state, but this is often infringed upon and results in disharmony. When any one religion seeks to dominate and control voting and laws that govern everyone, we move from diversity to division. There are protests in the streets and those on different sides of an issue become inflamed and sometime violent.

We further complicate matters by contradicting ourselves, speaking out of both sides of our mouths in relation to issues.

For example, in the state of Alabama, in a decision involving in-vitro fertilization and the protection of "extrauterine children," the Chief Justice of the Alabama Supreme Court said: "In summary, the theologically based view of the sanctity of life adopted by the People of Alabama encompasses the following (1) God made every person in His image; (2) each person therefore has a value that far exceeds the ability of human beings to calculate; and (3) human life cannot be wrongfully destroyed without incurring the wrath of a holy God, who views the destruction of His image as an affront to Himself."

These are very strong statements and yet the very same state of Alabama contradicts itself. It has one of the nation's highest per capita execution rates. It continues to allow the imposition of death sentences even when jury verdicts are not unanimous. For every eight people who have been executed, one has been exonerated. Does this not invoke the wrath of a holy God? Is this not the destruction of His image and an affront to Himself?

When we contradict ourselves, we play with verbiage and use it to justify what we want and to eliminate what we don't want. Given the position of the Alabama Supreme Court it might look at sanctity of life and take it to an extreme by condemning any male who engages in masturbation, or in sexual activity that is not solely focused on producing a child. Every man carries the seed of life, given by the God in whom the Chief Justice so fervently believes. To use that seed wantonly, to destroy life by ejaculating without fulfilling God's purpose, would, under the above thinking, be an affront to God.

Contradictions such as this are further examples of the state of polarities in which we currently continue to live. We twist meaning to satisfy our desires.

In the transformation that is coming, these differences will still exist because each cell is individual, but we will each make room for what is "other."

We can begin to do this in our current lives by developing curiosity about what is alien to us. To discover the wide variety that exists in belief systems and how carefully they have been structured by the elders so that theJy hold millions in their sway. Curiosity about the beliefs, the practices, the commitment, the rituals, the use of the liturgy to lift us into our highest and best and to help us merge with the Light when it is our time.

Yes. Curiosity will be a means to help us now to move from good *vs* evil to living in the Light. We will dare to expand ourselves beyond our comfort zone to stretch to other possibilities that exist beyond our ken. Everything that is, is there for us to explore as a possibility, as an alternative, to expand our knowledge of all that is.

We have not been able to do this because we cling to separation. In the new we will move beyond what limits us, beyond the barriers we have placed between us.

In my vision of the transformation, we will

approach all such issues from a grand perspective in which we hold a single overarching value: to celebrate all life unconditionally by committing as a human race to do no harm. What a different human race we will become. Now is the time to begin to shift our lives to unconditional love so that we will be ready for the new.

Love Will Lift Us

A major shift is coming. A transformation in which we will know we are each other. Life will be extraordinary when we come to know this. We will bring our talents and gifts to one another. We will enhance each other's lives. We will take each other's hands and warm each other.

We will not tell anyone anything. Instead, we will ask: What can you teach me? What do you know? How may I help? What may I give you?

And as we do that, we will rise like giants and accomplish feats we had no idea were possible. We will discover potential we never knew we had. We will care about each other to such a degree that love will lift us to unknown acts of creativity and possibility. This is who we shall become because we will know ourselves as cells in one body and we will become capable of all that awaits us in the Creative Force wherein there are no limits.

From PERSONAL To UNIVERSAL LOVE

When the transformation occurs, the way we love will shift as well. We will open beyond our small sphere of friends and family and realize that we can cherish all people equally. Even strangers.

I remember once standing in an elevator. Two others were in the same car, three strangers going up to their floors. One was an old woman, clinging to her purse, withdrawn into her thoughts. The other was a young man with ear buds and a tapping foot.

Of course, I knew nothing about either of these people, but I suddenly felt this rush of love from my heart center. I had no idea what evoked it, but I immediately knew that I could love these two as if they had been in my life all my life. I loved them just as they were. I didn't need to make them fit into my life as if they were relatives. I didn't need for the woman to take on the role of my mother or grandmother. I didn't need the chap to be my son or to remind me of fellows whom I dated when I was younger. I loved them because they were there in the elevator with me.

I had the fleeting thought that if the entire world were destroyed and only the three of us remained, I could love them as much as anyone I had ever loved in my life.

All at once it felt strange that I should be having such thoughts and simultaneously, it felt like the most normal act I could imagine.

I never said a word to either of them, but from that day forward, I knew I had made a shift from personal love to universal love, and I was eager to know more about it.

Universal Love

The way most of us live our lives in our current state of evolution, we have special people whom we love, other people we like and call friends, and an entire world of "others" who hold no place in our hearts. We invest considerable energy in the "special" people. They are family or mates or our children. They are important to us, and we would do anything for them. We often say we would protect them with our lives if necessary. We can't imagine our lives without them and if they die, we suffer and grieve.

We care equally for those we like and call them friends, but they are at a level below those we love. Often, we find that because the friends are on a lower rung, we sign letters to them, “affectionately” or “warmly” because “with love” is reserved for the more personal level. As for the others, mostly, we don’t care about them at all because we don’t know them and have not extended ourselves in their direction.

Anyone would say about the above assessment, “Well, of course. That’s the way life is. You can’t go around loving everyone equally. Who would even want to?”

The day in the elevator shifted me out of that way of thinking. I saw that when I directed love energy toward the special people in my life, I was creating a reality. I made them special and therefore they were. Knowing that, I saw that I could do that with anyone, make them special and pour my love out to them. Moreover, I could love anyone, and as deeply as I loved anyone. It was universal love, a step beyond the personal. It was to be “in love” (in a state of love) rather than to love a particular person. To be “in love” meant that love was activated in me through the heart center and that that love could be shared anywhere with anyone.

I knew there were people who lived this way. They were saints, like Mother Teresa. When she picked people up off the streets of India, she poured her heart center love into every one of them. No one was more important than any other. No one was less important than any other.

My spiritual mentor, Ev, taught me to be of service, to ask in all situations, how may I help? To reach out to everyone equally. To bring kindness and compassion to the world. I later took it as a daily objective: 'to be a blessing to everyone I meet.' These expressions were easy. But to love everyone equally, this was a step up.

Being of Service. Reaching out. Asking how I may help? Once the transformation has occurred, I see people all over the globe making the commitment to give of self in this way at least once every day. It will become a requirement of being alive. When enacted by millions, millions will be served every day and everyone who practices this will be acknowledging the privilege of giving from their uniqueness.

I loved my former acting teacher. She had been like a mother to me. In the last two years of her life, in her eighties, she lived alone in Northern California. As an expression of my love for her, I told her I would call her every day, so she could touch the outside world. I lived up to my commitment. It got to a point where if I was an hour later than usual, she would gently chide me, wondering if I had forgotten.

Calling her every day was a joy for me. It's not often we get to give someone such a meaningful gift. Toward the end of her life, she moved to a hospital. The last day I called her, her last words to me were, "I gotta go now, darlin'." I'll never forget the words or the privilege of loving someone so fully.

That was a very personal love. But now, awakened to universal love, I see that I could do that same thing with anyone who needed or wanted it. We wouldn't have to have history. I could do it because this would be another human being and I could love this being and call every day.

Knowing this, I feel lifted to the next level of living. It is exhilarating. It is what life will be like when the coming transformation occurs. Love will flow from person to person, and everyone will be made whole. Here is a perfect example of what I am referring to:

Sarena Diamond wrote of her experience which she called "An Opportunity to Give."

"I flew home to NYC last night, tired but

feeling fulfilled knowing the work week had been so impactful and progressive for my client.

"I was on the phone with my love while walking toward the parking garage, so I almost missed the young woman who cowered in a corner by the escalator. She was sitting on her suitcase, talking on the phone, and crying hard. I put my call on hold and took two steps back and asked, 'Sweetie, are you okay?'

"Long story short, she wasn't okay. She'd been stranded for 7 hours, crying on the phone with her mom in the Midwest (where she had flown from) because neither of them knew what to do. She was moving back to the Catskills (about 3 hours from JFK by car) and her ride never showed up. She didn't have the know-how to navigate NYC transit to get her someplace where she might have gotten a train. And she didn't have money or a credit card to get a return flight. She was literally stranded in the airport with no idea what to do and she was so scared (those fake Uber drivers that roam the airport scare even me sometimes). I spoke to the mom who was sobbing on the other end of the phone line and told her I would do what I could to help her daughter.

"The week had been an emotional one for me, so helping someone else's adult kid filled my heart with a tiny bit of comfort. I opened my Uber account and arranged a ride to take her safely where she needed to be. I talked with her several times on the phone to know that she was calmer, and the driver was courteous to her.

"I drove home thinking that a thousand people must have walked by over the hours she was stranded, ignoring the scared tears of an 18-year-old. How fortunate am I to have had the opportunity to show caring to a young adult who is just starting her life, and alleviate worry for that mom a thousand miles from her baby?

"I'm feeling blessed by the opportunity to help someone in need. I pray that halfway across the world, there are caring people who will offer comfort for the families and friends of those US military members, and my boy, as the needs unfold."

Functioning from the Heart Center (Chakra)

I loved how Sarena had opened her heart center and made herself fully available to help and resolve the crisis. And when she thought of the thousand people who had simply walked past the girl, Sarena didn't criticize them. Instead, she did what was there for her to do. She was being the change she wanted to see happen[1] and she expressed love for the girl as if she had been her own child.

As we practice expressing Universal Love, we will learn, that what we receive will come from what we have given.

Until now in the evolutionary process, love has been thought of as something over which we have no jurisdiction. Our experience is that love is bigger than we are, and we can't know when it will awaken in relation to another. We meet someone and suddenly we begin to have stirrings. Those just come and we feel enlivened in a new way and drawn to this person.

What we know about love is that it is a powerful, complex emotional experience that involves changes in our body chemistry, including our neurotransmitters (brain chemicals). It impacts our social relationships in varied ways, affecting how we relate to others around us.

When we are transformed, we will gain a deeper knowing of the function of the heart center. Love will not have its origins in the solar plexus as a feeling. Instead, it will begin in the heart center and will radiate out from there

---

1 One of the six Love Principles.

with warmth and light. While the sensation might start on its own in relation to someone who comes into our field, we will have the power to guide and direct the love energy that is emanating from us. Once we can do this, we will be able to instantly configure that love energy as compassion, or empathy, or forgiveness, or desire, or comfort, or encouragement, or praise. We will be able to determine the intensity of the emission and temper it at will.

If we are awakening love energy in relation to a child or a single individual, we will be able to create a flow that does not overwhelm but rather awakens in the recipient a sense of safety and of being cared for. If we are in a scene of crisis, we will be able to expand the intensity to cover the whole range of focus and send forth an expression powerful enough to shift the emotions that predominate and disturb. The chaos will be disarmed by the force of love that is now surrounding it and the change of frequency will become evident to all present because of the impact and imprint. It will be a light permeating the darkness.

This power of love that will awaken in all of us in the coming transformation has already been evidenced by those rare individuals who have already experienced the awakening.

In the summer of 1982, a war raged between Israel and the Palestine Liberation Organization. At the height of the siege, Mother Teresa traveled to the midst of the war zone on a mission. She had come to evacuate 37 retarded and handicapped children from a mental hospital in the Sabra refugee camp.

She was told that there was no way she could proceed as heavy fighting was in progress. Teresa held to her purpose, sent forth heart center love energy to all those who were present, and brokered a temporary cease-fire between the Israeli army and the Palestinian guerrillas. Accompanied by Red Cross workers, she then traveled through the war zone to evacuate the young patients. The children were taken to the Spring School in east Beirut, an institution founded by Mother Teresa two years before.

Lucy Stevenson Ewell wrote up the whole story for Church magazines. It is worth sharing here because it would seem impossible that Teresa could have intervened in this way amid fierce fighting and killing. But in fact, she did.

"Mother Teresa was a woman who loved serving God and helping people. She was called 'Mother' because she was a nun in her church. When she was 18, she moved to India and started teaching children there. When they didn't have paper or pencils, she drew the alphabet in the dirt with a stick. She also took care of people who were sick or poor. For many years, she lived with them and tried to help them.

"She knew God loved all people. And she spent her whole life loving and helping them.

"When Mother Teresa was 72 years old, a war started in Lebanon. Someone told her that there were some children who were stranded in a hospital there and needed help. Many of them couldn't walk or talk. They didn't have any food to eat. And they were afraid because of the war going on outside the hospital. The children needed help getting to a safe place.

"Mother Teresa wanted to help these children. So she traveled to Lebanon. When she got there, she talked with some men to make a plan.

"'We need to rescue the children in the hospital,' she said.

"'That's a good idea,' one of the men said. 'But it's too dangerous.'

"Mother Teresa probably looked small standing next to the men. But her faith was great and strong. 'I believe it is our duty,' she said.

"'But do you hear the bombs?' another man

asked.

"'Yes, I hear them.'

"'It's absolutely impossible to go to the hospital now,' he said. 'You simply cannot go unless the fighting stops.'

"Mother Teresa smiled a kind smile. 'I prayed,' she said. 'I'm sure the fighting will stop long enough for us to help the children.'

"The men were surprised by Mother Teresa's faith. They agreed that if it was safe, they would take her to the hospital the next day.

"When Mother Teresa woke early the next morning, everything was quiet. There were no bombs. The fighting had stopped. It was safe to rescue the children! She left right away.

"Mother Teresa led a group of helpers to the hospital. When she walked inside, the children were huddled together in the middle of the room. They were scared. Some of them were crying.

"Mother Teresa walked quietly toward them and gave hugs to the little ones. Even the children who were most afraid felt safe in her arms. She shook hands with the older children. Her hands were wrinkled, but gentle and warm.

"She knew God loved these children. And she loved them too.

"One by one, Mother Teresa and the helpers carried the children out of the hospital. They wrapped them in warm blankets. They put them gently into ambulances. Then they drove them to a safe place where more people could help them.

"The next day, the bombs and fighting started again. But the children were safe!"

In 1979, Mother Teresa was awarded the Nobel Peace Prize. In her Nobel Lecture, she said: "I think that we in our family don't need bombs and guns, to destroy to bring peace – just get together, love one another, bring that peace, that joy, that strength of presence of each other in the home. And we will be able to overcome all the evil that is in the world."

The Power of Universal Love

For Mother Teresa, it was God who stopped the fighting and the bombing so that she could do His work and bring the children to safety. Was it God? Or was it the power of her love that parted the blood-stained battlefield and held the combatants at bay? If God is Love, it matters not which it was, only that it was.

What will the coming transformation bring? Universal love will illumine the darkness. For starters, millions of people will awaken every day with the purpose of loving at least one stranger and everyone else who crosses their path. There will be such an abundance of love energy that problems will find open pathways to the opportunities they represent. Healing of physical illnesses will occur more rapidly in the presence of heart center flow. Men, women, and children will smile and fill with joy as they go about their lives because they will have been loved and they will have loved, universally.

Those who remain in the shadows and seek to bash the world with their need for power and their debasement of life will hit the wall of their own hate and find it hard to get up again. But they will be helped up repeatedly by those embodying Universal Love, and eventually they will turn from their harshness and open to the possibility that goodness is prevailing, that it is deterring and detouring their negativity. They will change or they will fade away, locked in the prison of their own misdeeds, afraid of being blinded by the prevailing light.

Universal love encourages us to seek out the unusual and to find beauty in all life, in people, and in customs that are completely different from our own.

The Love Principle *Receive All People as Beautiful Exactly as They Are* exemplifies this. The melting pot of the United States has whites, Blacks, Latinos, Asians, Indigenous, etc., young, and old, as well as all manner of sexual identities, professions, and religious affiliations.

To receive all people requires breathing, so the passages of welcome can open. It can occur only through the heart center, an open love channel that is unconditionally receptive. All people cannot be received through the head or the mind because they will run into the interference of thoughts, opinions, and most especially judgments.

All people means everyone; none is more valuable than any other. None is lesser than any other. *Receive all people as beautiful. Beautiful* means in their perfection. Each is a unique individual bringing their special gifts to the whole. Each contributes in a different way. Each is needed as if they are a puzzle piece in a grand mosaic called humanity.

Receive All People as Beautiful Exactly as They Are. Exactly as they are, not as I or you would have them be. Not as I or you would change them (which we couldn't do, in any case.) *Exactly as they are* because that is the contribution they are making to the whole and that contribution is needed and to be cherished. A carousel that is missing its horses is lesser indeed. A locked door without a keyhole is troublesome. An egg carton with 11 eggs disrupts omelets. A baseball team without a pitcher is useless. A sea of white faces without contrast is a colorless blur.

Joy Bodies

Once Universal Love takes hold, love will combine with joy and the air will be electric with a level of happiness never before known. So many people will be loving so many people every day that we will all find our capacity for love and joy expanded exponentially. Glowing faces will greet glowing faces and we will all be infused with Light. People will break out into smiles for no reason, begin to do a little dance step while walking, or start singing as they walk along. It will be a result of love, gladness, and utter joy spilling over because there will be too much of it to contain.

Over 50 years ago I started having the spillover sensation. The image that came was that I was beside myself with joy. To allow the love and joy I was experiencing to continue without interruption, I created an imaginary "Joy Body" to walk beside me. It was like having a blowup replica of myself that bounded along with each step I took. It housed the joy that I thought was too much for me to maintain and stay on the ground at the same time. After a few years, I was able to expand my being sufficiently to sustain the ecstasy within myself and to send it forth in greater abundance.

When I talk about the spill-over sensation, if you envision an overly friendly dog, you will see what I mean. Some dogs love everyone. When they wag their tails, they wag their whole bodies. They can't contain what they feel. They pull on their leash. They want to greet the stranger who is approaching. They jump and bark a greeting. They lick the hand extended to them. They cannot stop expressing themselves because there is so much to express.

The joy I feel today as I express Universal Love appears in my eyes as a constant radiance, ever present but not overwhelming. It comes forth like a laser piercing the air and traveling as a beam to everyone I meet.

I am thrilled to know that when the coming transformation occurs people everywhere will be filled with and expressive of Universal Love and that it will bring continuous joy to everyone they meet.

Gone will be the days of multitudes seeing

no one as they walk the earth making no connection with the people they pass (the other cells in the body of the whole.) How much we miss today with our immovable faces and our constrained lives. How we limit ourselves if we don't know that Universal Love longs to awaken in us.

There are whole cultures in our world where people naturally share their love with everyone. Most of these are comprised of Indigenous people who, much more than white or western folks, value making eye contact and touching heart to heart. These are people who don't have much on the material plane but are far more wealthy in quality of life than their counterparts who live in abundance and disconnect from the whole.

A walk down any alleyway in India unites us person to person, eye to eye, heart center to heart center with a smile and a namaste. It is as if we all belong to one billion 400 million close relatives in a love family!

Because I have experienced the greeting of those in the world who know how to connect heart to heart and because I know myself what it is to overflow with love and joy throughout the day, I can have a tiny inkling of what it will be like following the coming transformation, when the influence of the cosmos impacts the frequency of Planet Earth and we are all lifted into finer frequencies we have never before known, and the population of over 8 billion people begins to radiate the blessing of Universal Love to each other and to everyone.

In the simplest terms it will be as if everyone moved, as in the song, to the sunny side of the street! In its greater meaning it will mean that expressions such as war, violence, hate, and the like will have no chance to survive, having been overrun, overtaken, by a force so great that nothing lesser is acceptable.

From COMPETITION To COOPERATION

Competition is a form of inspiration. It makes us strive to be better than others, to accomplish more, to be the best, to make great profit, to win awards. Competition is also a form of us-*vs*-them. A transformation in consciousness in relation to competition will take us to levels that will serve everyone equally and lift the competition to new and more exciting levels.

Every year I watch award shows where performing artists compete for best this and best that. When people win in their category, they very often salute their opponents, say they are in excellent company, and that all of them are equally deserving. They are correct in this assessment.

In these award shows, excellence is celebrated; first with a nomination and then with choosing one for the award. The entire process is arbitrary and subjective. When choosing the best actor, for example, there are multiple factors at play. There is skill: how well were they able to execute the role they were playing? There is artistry: did they "play themselves" or did they create a character different from how they function in their "real" life? There is character development: did they change their physical expression, their speech, their voice? There is box office: did they draw audience in and create a financial success?

And all of this is subjective because the theme and material from one film to another is different and has different audience appeal. And it is subjective because of how the actor was guided by the director, provided for by the writers, enhanced by the production, enabled by budget, helped by distribution, etc. In addition, there is face recognition, reputation, star power, and the privilege of having been cast in the first place.

When the presenter says, And the winner is...what criteria went into that choice and how can we know that "Best Actor for a Performance in a Film" was the best actor? We don't. We know that someone was singled out and chosen from among the many who were equally deserving.

In the next stage of our development, in the coming transformation, we will not choose one winner. Instead, we will give each nominee an award for a particular dimension that made them shine enough to be selected as nominees.

An example of this would be an Academy Award for Lighting Design. If there were five nominees, each of them would be a winner for the specific that lifts the production of the film to a new level. That would be the goal, not who is the "best for lighting design." It could be delineated as follows: 1. For highlighting a pivotal turning point. 2. For enhancing a moment. 3. For embellishing an emotion. 4. Illuminating the theme. 5. Creating an illusion.

In this way, all the nominees are the winners, and for different criteria. It hones the award, stresses a particular expression of excellence, and lifts the whole of the craft in the process.

In the area of sports, it is easier to determine a winning team than a winning actor or lighting designer. At the end of the game there is a score. But is the winning team the best team? Again, there are too many factors at play: location, weather, team spirit on that day, condition of the field, calls by the referees, pressure imposed by the opposition, favoritism, fan support, etc.

In our current world both in performance art and in sports, the almighty dollar has assumed a prominent role. Millions of dollars are paid out to players in both areas and millions of dollars are invested in the productions. The cost is passed on to the fans in the charge for admission. Personal benefit accrues for the lead players in future contracts, in fame, in personal wealth and personal glory. Children look up to heroes and strive to obtain a piece of the action when they grow up. While there is nothing wrong with any of this, the motivation is inferior because it focuses on the personal rather than the universal. It is focused on reward rather than elevating excellence.

Competition will experience an upgrade in the coming transformation, a move from being on top to *raising the level of what the top means*. I am speaking of stretching the self to heights never reached, thus tapping into more of individual potential or moving from good to better, to great, to beyond great.

The sport of golf, also a big business, comes close to lifting competition to this next level. While players compete against each other for "jackets" and big dollar prizes, they mostly compete against the course, the current conditions, and their own history. They seek with every stroke to play a perfect hole, to use all their accumulated skill, to hold a focus, to direct the trajectory of the ball. Each round is an endeavor to raise the level of what the top means, to score as much under par as possible with the best form possible.

In the case of golf, while competition against other players is in place, the deeper focus is on moment-to-moment excellence, making every movement count, and exceeding one's own personal best. This can also be said of swimming, of gymnastics, of skiing, and figure skating. Yes, all the participants are competing against one another for “gold,” but they are stretching themselves to exceed their own capacities, to reach beyond to yet unrecorded excellence.

This lifting of competition to the next level is about expanding human potential, competing with former human achievements, and achieving more than we ever thought possible. It is a way of acknowledging that we have scratched only the surface of our potential.

This is also where cooperation comes into the picture with competition. When each individual, each team, each genre, holds as their focus of competition the desire to become the greater human expression that awaits and beckons, then each will cooperate with the other to find ways for humans to stretch to this new. The purpose will be collective human growth. Each individual unit will work toward encouraging every other unit to take new steps and open new vistas.

The goal will not be to do it first, or to do it better than the other, but to do it for the good of the whole. Each will share their incremental steps of discovery and achievement. Everyone will benefit from everyone’s steps and apply shared learning. Greed will be replaced by interconnected economics.

Looking at competition between companies, for electronics, or vehicles, or appliances, or clothing, or communications, or anything, rather than seeking to outdo the competitors, to become top of the field, to make the most profit, the focus will be on moving from being on top to raising the level of what the top means.

We already have smart phones that use GPS as an alert system should the user fall. Competitors scramble to get that on to their system. Yet, if all companies worked together to raise the level of performance, we might develop phones that could do instant x-rays or even apply healing technology that would treat the injured on the spot. It is not beyond the realm of possibility, nothing is. Astounding advances will more easily be achieved when innovators all work together to pool their genius for the good of the whole world.

When this occurs, there will still be different brands in relation to colors offered or size or unique style, but the focus of the innovation in technology will be on developing the finest tool possible and having it benefit everyone.

Excellence, Surpassing Ourselves

Competition is our current stimulant for improving and developing our skills. The focus on excellence is the next step. When our attention is directed to excellence, the process of inner achievement is awakened. With each advance we will feel drawn to the more and we will be thrilled by each accomplishment, no matter how small or by whom. Next, we will begin to move toward perfection. Perfection will represent our application of improvement until we arrive at a flawless state, as faultless as possible. But perfection is not the end. It is only the best that is possible in the moment we evaluate it. It is the farthest accomplishment we can imagine.

In the new frequency we will transcend our imagination and open to a realm of creativity which surpasses anything we have previously known. That is part of the transformation that will occur. Knowing this it becomes easier to see how the lesser, which represents life today, will simply fall away. There is no limit to where we are headed. Just as we cannot fathom the endless universe that stretches out before us, we cannot imagine what lies beyond perfection.

This focus will move us from good to great.

Every arena of life will be affected when our focus shifts in this way, when we cooperate with each other and redefine the goal of reaching the top or being the best. In world affairs we will not focus on living in peace together but rather on innovation. We will already be living in peace because we will have moved beyond the wastefulness of self-protection, the lunacy of war and killing, nationalism and flag-waving, even borders.

Humanity will be enthralled by its potential and all energy will be directed to developing that potential and making it a reality so that we move from any form of deprivation to exhilaration over accomplishment and possibility. Everyone will make their unique contribution to the whole that serves everyone equally. We will come to equally value those who run corporations and those who are laborers, those who sit behind mahogany desks and those who pick crops in the fields. One without the other is not as strong as both seen as enabling life to thrive.

Humans have had and shared sporadic moments of exhilaration. Moments of utter joy, or endless possibility. I was a child when World War 2 ended, and I have never forgotten the rejoicing in the streets and the pulling of the shades to allow the light to enter. It was as if a mammoth burden had been lifted from everyone's back and they could lift to their full height in freedom with no limits in front of them.

When the millennium turned to 2000, a world united in excitement sent up brilliant fireworks from every nation and time zone. Something grand was taking place on the planet and we were all a part of it together. We were all connected with something greater than ourselves and promise beat loudly in every heart.

We have rejoiced in expressions of greatness like listening to deeply inspiring music, or looking into the Mona Lisa, or standing at the feet of the statue of David or cheering at the conclusion of a brilliantly played sports event. We unite in a way that defies explanation. We smile. We feel blessed. The joy is contagious. We are closer to the Divine in the ecstasy we create. And we feel there is no limit on how high we can go. We do this together and therein lies the power of rising above the status quo, of moving from good to great.

We all have a glimmer of what our world could be like if we reached out to each other and joined with one another. When the coming transformation begins, we will go beyond reaching and joining. We will know we are One being and the creative power that awaits us will illumine our great life.

We will leave behind the soap opera of self-created woes such as struggles for power, causes and beliefs that conflict with one another, fear, and the need for protection, and all those "things" we have labeled as "important." We created these realities to manufacture meaning because we had not yet touched what is greater than all we struggle with on this plane of consciousness. We created darkness so we could strive for light.

Now is the time to walk forward and become a link between the lesser we have known and nurtured and the more that is calling, to become those who praise life and devote self to the single cause of elevating humanity to union with the Divine.

In the Hebrew tradition, on the High Holy Days, there is the practice of *teshuvah.* It means to "turn around." It is part of the process of repentance, but more than that, it is the literal and figurative struggle to return to God. It is coming home with a full heart and soul and that return involves a changing of the heart and ways of living.

If we think of God as the Divine Light, *Teshuvah* encourages consciously turning away from lesser ways of functioning and lifting self into finer frequencies. When we function beneath our potential as beings, the Light is at our back inspiring us to awaken. But when we "turn around" to face the Radiance and absorb it into ourselves so that we might reflect it back, we become more of who we are meant to be. Our imprint overall then helps to lift humanity to rebirth.

From FEAR TO AWE

Fear is an emotion that will undergo transformation in the emerging human. It is an instinctive expression that stunts our ability to soar.

As we prepare for the coming transformation, we can begin to look at how we create fear and how we can move beyond that limiting emotion. In our current state of development, fear is part of human nature and can be appropriate when we sense danger. Yet, all too often, fear is created in relation to something we don't want to happen rather than something that might hurt us. We protect ourselves from what "might" come. We retreat, hold our breath, and tense our bodies as we try to stave off the unwanted.

Fear is characterized by "stopping," or freezing in place, by inhibiting our life force. We immobilize ourselves. In that regard it can be said to be more frightening than what might be coming because we have choked back our energy and rendered ourselves ineffective.

We sometimes take this to the next step, anxiety. This goes beyond fear in the moment to the debilitating anticipation of what might happen in the future. This leads to negative thinking or worry. Worry is particularly meaningless. It is solely based on "ifs" and "mights," none of which are occurring. All such behavior is non-productive and diminishing of human potential.

In the realm of feelings, fear is one of the most useless in decision-making, in relationships, and in health matters. In decision-making, there is fear of making the wrong choice. If I make the wrong choice, it is not the end of the world. I can always make a new choice. While the same opportunity might not be in front of me, other opportunities will be there instead. It is the nature of life. Creating fear about deciding muddies the waters, and it takes the joy out of the decision I do make.

Fear about entering a relationship puts a damper on it before it even begins. If I fear initiating something with someone new even before starting it, I will have already affected what will emerge between us because I have limited its possibilities with my own hesitation.

Fear in relation to health matters can easily worsen the condition because how I feel emotionally has a direct effect on what manifests physically. I have watched people fear that they will "catch" whatever is "going around," and sure enough they do "catch" it because they unknowingly opened receptivity to the condition by focusing so much attention on it

Beyond Ordinary Thinking

In the coming transformation humanity will be elevated from fear to awe. There are many elements involved in making the shift. Going beyond ordinary thinking is one.

When I was diagnosed with breast cancer in 2010, the ordinary thinking of the day was to "fight" the disease, fight it with every weapon at your disposal, and stamp it out. The temptation to fear was great. What if this and what if that?

I took a deep breath and rejected both fighting the cancer and conjecture. I could see that fear would not serve me. I took many deep breaths looking for an alternative way to relate to the cancer. As I opened to possibilities, I could feel my consciousness lifting. It was as if I was pulling up a shade of gloom that had descended. I could feel light coming into my field. I was shifting from fear to awe.

I became curious about cells that were growing inside my breast. They had taken up residence and were busy being creative. I knew I needed to rid myself of them. I did not need to create fear of them. Nor did I put up resistance to them.

In the shift to awe, I saw that I could embrace them rather than consider them enemies. I would not fight them because I would then be fighting myself since they now were part of my body. As the light of possibility continued to rise in me, I saw an opportunity. I began talking to the cells and asking them to go to sleep, to go dormant, to cease reproduction, to remain contained and not spread elsewhere in my body or lymph nodes.

I had a grand interaction with them, an intimate relationship. I embraced them with love and compassion because I knew that they were going to be surgically removed during the mastectomy treatment I had chosen. I wasn't fearful because I was now directing my inner healing process.

I told the cells that I didn't want to hurt them, but that it was not healthy for me to have them live in my breast. I expressed compassion for them and told them I hoped they suffered no pain when they were removed. I created a cooperative relationship with them, a mutual sense of caring. I created no resistance. As a result, I never had any pain throughout the entire process. When the breast tissue was removed, it was revealed that the cells had not multiplied, nor had they spread anywhere.

I was in awe of how the process had worked and I was filled with gratitude, a steady flow of it each day. That gratitude continues as

I rise each morning to greet each new day. Fear of the cancer would not have served me.

Fear in relation to anything does not serve. On a world level, fear can be devastating because it can provoke unnecessary destructive and precipitous actions based on irrational anticipation of what others might do.

Reverence for the Unknown

In the coming transition, human beings will choose awe over fear. Just saying the word awe, shifts the facial expression of the one speaking. Fear thrusts the mouth forward and furrows the brow. Awe opens the mouth as if singing, opens the eyes wider, and lifts the eyebrows in wonder. This is an indication of how it opens the energy field to welcome the unknown and to move forward into greater potential with curiosity and excitement.

Awe awakens reverence for the unknown. Opening to that enables us to stand in the presence of something vast and mysterious, something we don't know, something that challenges how we have seen the world. As we yield to what we can't see, we enter a field that is grand, sublime, powerful, and much larger than ourselves or our thinking. Awe opens the door to limitless vastness, to the Cosmos and all it has to offer.

To live in awe, we must welcome the unknown and to do that we must cease seeking to control. The great joke is that none of us has control even though we think we do. *We have control over nothing. Life unfolds in harmony with Itself, not in accordance with the demands we place on it.*

It is a relief to learn this because our daily lives require much less effort when we don't try to control outcomes. Instead of strategizing and seeking to manipulate, we simply enter the flow, bring our hopes and dreams, and apply our talents as we watch realities emerge. It is a whole different way of being.

I have shifted into awe countless times in my life and the results have been extraordinary. Now, I envision what it will be like to live this 100% of the time as I transform.

Having Abundant Expectancy

When switching from fear to awe, a good practice is to *have no expectations, but rather abundant expectancy.*

To have an expectation is to try to limit what may occur. We want something to turn out a certain way. If it doesn't, we will be disappointed. If it does turn out the way we wanted, we might be happy, but we will not know what might have emerged had we not imposed ourselves on the unknown.

The picture we formed of what we wanted to happen emerged from the small perspective of what we already know. But beyond that is an entire realm of possibilities. By having abundant expectancy, we open ourselves to that mysterious realm and invite ourselves to be surprised by what might emerge.

Expectations are fixed views. Abundant expectancy is akin to sitting on the very edge of a chair and opening to the new that is ready to manifest. It opens the whole world to us. Fear leads us to hold an expectation that would be comfortable. Awe takes us beyond our limited selves to merge with a greater reality that has no limits.

Have no expectations but rather abundant expectancy is one of The Love Principles which I originated in November 1970. How these principles came into being is an example of how moving past fear can lead to an awesome experience, in this case one that completely changed my life direction and resulted in changing the lives of multitudes.

I was teaching in a ghetto high school in Brooklyn, N.Y. Nothing about it was easy. No need to dwell here on what was wrong. One day, I broke up a fight that bordered on a riot during an auditorium program. I did it by moving past my fear of what was occurring. I knew I needed to act immediately. I jumped up out of my chair and rushed into chaos. I stood between the boys and sent them love energy. I had entered a flow larger than myself, a state of awe.

The boys turned and walked away and the crowd calling for blood dispersed. I stood trembling. I knew that I had participated in a small miracle. I had enabled a transformation. I knew that what I had done was the result of studying the Ancient Wisdom, attending "classes" in my sleep which prepared me for being a vessel for love, and making a commitment to being my highest and best in every moment. Later, my students and I wept together over the troublesome circumstances that hovered over our school every day. We wanted to make a difference and we made a commitment to finding our way to that.

When I returned to my office, the state of awe continued. A Ray of Light came through a solid wall. I heard an inner voice tell me that I was to initiate The Love Project and I was given six Love Principles by which to live. I immediately put the gift I had received into practice, having no idea whatsoever what The Love Project would be, what I would do, who, if anyone, on staff would join me. There was no fear. I had yielded to the momentum, to the flow that was the emerging reality.

The Love Principle that started everything rolling was *Be the Change*. This principle has become ubiquitous. I am humbled to have originated it (even though it ended up being wrongly attributed to Mahatma Gandhi.) The whole of the principle was *Be The Change You Want To See Happen, Instead Of Trying To Change Anyone Else.*

To move to a state of awe, to *Be the Change*, I first needed to know what change I wanted to see. What did I want to bring into being?

I wanted students to know that I cared about them. I wanted them to have something to look forward to in their mostly deprived and difficult lives.

At a faculty meeting that very afternoon, I announced that I would be conducting a Love Project and that I intended to turn the school around into a place of learning, and love, and even joy. Two teachers said they would join me; most of the others called me Alice in Wonderland.

We stirred the interest of the student body by putting signs all over the building saying, "The Seekers are coming." Two weeks later we went into every homeroom and delivered to each student two cookies we had baked in the home economics department of the school. My goal had been to bring a little sweetness to their lives. I also knew many came to school hungry.

The result of this first effort immediately changed the energy in the entire building. The bell rang and students were smiling, and talking about the event as they went to their classes. Joy and delight filled the hallways.

Creating a Love Project

This one small beginning led the way to several Love Project expressions over the next seven months. The school went through a metamorphosis during that time. We created powerful change. LOOK Magazine sent a reporter and photographer to cover the story, as did local newspapers.

The Love Project enabled me to give life to the other five Love Principles as well. *Create Your Own Reality Consciously, Have No Expectations but Rather Abundant Expectancy, Provide Others with Opportunities to Give, Receive All People as Beautiful Exactly As They Are,* and *Problems Are Opportunities.*

For the next 53-years and still counting, my partner Diane K. Pike and I have been teaching and disseminating The Love Principles. They have made their way around the world multiple times over and they have helped countless people to change their lives for the better, to expand their consciousness, and to be ready for this new evolutionary step that is waiting to come into being.

If I had stymied myself with fear, stayed in my seat, and not gone to stop that fight, none of the above would have happened. When the fight broke out, I didn't think "Should I go?"

I didn't wonder, in fear, what would happen to me if I intervened. Instead, with a clear mind free of worry and an open-heart center, I jumped up and rushed into the conflict. Standing in the turbulence between the two boys, I again felt no fear. I directed my love energy outward instead. As the chaos disintegrated, I stood trembling. I had moved into awe, awe of the power of love.

From 1970 on I lived my life with a focus on awe and what it would next bring into my life. A neighbor's son died, and I heard his mother lamenting her loss. "Why me?" she cried. I had heard those words thousands of times in my life but when I listened from that vast space of awe, I heard the lament as a legitimate question. A question not filled with regret but rather asking a real question. Why has this befallen me? What is it asking of me? What is it teaching me? What new is it bringing to me? Two weeks later I had written a book, "Why Me? How to Heal What's Hurting You." This could never have occurred had I not opened in awe to all that waited in the universe.

When living in fear we put a damper on our lives. We are mired in concerns that might never eventuate. We hold ourselves back. When we shift into viewing life as a glorious mystery waiting to unfold, every moment is filled with wonder and possibility. We don't "tell" life anything or seek to impose our will upon it. Instead, we are in a constant state of asking, what's next? What am I not seeing? What is awaiting me? What more is being asked of me?

When the transformation comes, and every one of us does this, and we all dip into the potential that lies hidden in us, we will call forth incredible new expressions that will benefit the whole of the world around us. As it is now, too many of us trudge along, living patterned lives, not expanding who we are but focusing on getting through the day and not making waves.

There are the few among us who live in awe and who innovate, who invent, who see through the veil of normalcy to the more that awaits us. They see it and they bring it into being so we might all benefit.

It is time for the few who see and do this to become the many. Let's not wait for the transformation. Let's begin practicing now. Each of us has special gifts waiting to be unwrapped. Insights, talents, and visions that need to be awakened. All this will soon become the new reality and the world will be flooded with innovation born of a population newly in love with awe. Humanity will no longer cower in fear. Incredible potential and creativity will be released.

A Life-Altering Program

In 1981, I felt a former self calling to me. It was the me who had been a professional actor and director for 18 years. I listened to it with no expectations. I knew I didn't want to return to a career in the theatre, but because it was calling it was incumbent upon me to listen, to see what new might be there. I didn't create fear in myself that whatever was calling might disrupt the work I was already doing. I didn't want to leave that work. I loved my life as it was, but something was niggling at me, demanding my attention.

I breathed deeply and asked *what was wanted of me.* Then I proceeded one small step at time, without fear. I was led to return to my theatre books and to reread some of Constantine Stanislavsky. I had been taught his techniques and used them as an actor. At the beginning of one of his books, I read that he encouraged readers to take his work to the next level, to go beyond what he had created. I breathed again and asked the same question, what is wanted of me? To what next level might I take Stanislavsky's powerful contributions?

My former actor-self joined forces with myself as teacher of Ancient Wisdom and facilitator of personal growth. I was led to create a life-altering program called The Theatre of

Life. I took all the techniques I had once used to create roles for the stage and applied them to "real" life so that participants could consciously create "the character they were playing." This led participants to break through to entirely new ways of thinking and living.

For example, in Theatre of Life, individuals learned that they are not the personality/ character who makes an entrance on life's stage each day. In fact, they are the Player who, when they are conscious, can create any personality/character they wish! If they preferred quiet shyness and simply lived that way because that is who they thought they were, they could, upon awakening, create an ebullient, enthusiastic, full-voiced, fully participating person and take that self out into their regular world, playing that role guided by Player consciousness and direction. Imagine how that would utterly surprise people in their lives who knew them the other way!

For twenty-one years my partner and I had the privilege of watching people discover that they could create their daily lives consciously. I get reports to this day of how people are using what they learned in the Theatre of Life program to bring greater expression to their daily lives. It is awesome.

Fear is inhibiting. Opening instead to awe is exhilarating and without a ceiling. Leaving fear behind, the vista ahead of us is filled with light and we can step forward from good to great because we hold nothing back. Our world will know no boundaries to creativity when the coming transformation lifts us all into a state of awe.

From BELIEF To KNOWING

When the coming transformation in consciousness occurs, humans will shift from beliefs to knowing. This will be one of the major changes that will occur, and it will lead to very different ways of living.

Humanity has lived in the Age of Belief, also known as the Piscean Age, for a long time, about 2600 years. A major characteristic of this period is that humans have relied on beliefs and belief systems to give meaning to their lives. Beliefs are feelings, impressions, notions, opinions, and things we cling to and say, "this exists" (whether it does or not.) We believe that it does, and we place our confidence in it. We take it as true. Beliefs line up with our attitudes and how our minds function. Beliefs are wholly subjective, can't necessarily be proven, but we accept them and say, "this is so."

In 1953, Ervin Drake, Al Stillman, Jimmy Shirl, and Rivin Graham wrote a song called "I Believe." The lyrics were very uplifting. They created a reality that good was in the world and that it would always be so.

"I believe for every drop of rain that falls

A flower grows

I believe that somewhere in the darkest night

A candle glows

I believe for everyone who goes astray, someone will come

To show the way

I believe

I believe

I believe above a storm the smallest prayer

Can still be heard

I believe that someone in the great somewhere

Hears every word

Every time I hear a new born baby cry,

Or touch a leaf or see the sky

Then I know why, I believe."

The song is filled with faith that we are watched over, cared about, and cared for. It speaks of the ever-present light in the darkness.

Beliefs sustain us, guide us, encourage us. They can be good, wholesome, and nourishing. And yet, we need to examine our beliefs and our belief systems to make sure they are valid and life-affirming. Belief is one degree below knowing, and that one degree leads to a profound difference in human living.

As we progress from belief to knowing, we will continue to value beliefs that have served us, especially in our spiritual life. However, as we shift to finer frequency living, we will look at each belief we hold to see if we know in our deepest selves that this belief is true and valid. Knowing will supersede believing.

Belief is often limiting, and it creates separations. Knowing is inclusive. It benefits the whole. Knowing derives from a source greater than self.

An Exploration of Belief

Beliefs begin in us when we are very young. We are influenced by our parents and their beliefs, by our teachers, and by our young friends. Beliefs have a magnetic quality to them. It is easy for us to attach to them. In the case of our childhood friends, we value what they value because this further cements the closeness we have. We don't want to be different if we can help it.

Kids often raise questions like, "Do you believe there is a God?" Neither friend really knows if God exists, but they tend to decide together what they will believe. It is akin to their choosing a favorite game and believing that it is their favorite game.

Beliefs emerge out of what is important to us. When my partner Diane was a little girl, she utterly adored her grandfather. When he died, she saw him in his casket, and then the casket was buried. She had heard in Sunday School that people who were buried would be resurrected when Gabriel came and blew his horn. Diane couldn't picture her granddad having to wait in the cold ground for Gabriel to blow his horn. So, she and her best friend Jody decided not to believe that this could be true, especially about Diane's grandfather.

At the tender age of 7, Diane and Jody began to delineate between what to believe or not to believe. That is the nature of beliefs; there is a choice in relation to them. What fits with the believer's values? In this case, sitting on a haystack in the Nebraska sun, two children made their world a more comfortable place by choosing what to believe.

As we age and identify with groups, we gravitate toward whole belief systems. Consensus confirms the beliefs held and beliefs are received as truths.

If persons of the Jewish faith who believe in God trust that fasting and repenting on Yom Kippur will absolve them of their sins and inscribe their name in the Book of Life, for them, it will indeed be so. They will believe that God has forgiven them, and they can go forward cleansed. Catholics have a similar system of being absolved through confession.

Have they really been absolved? And by whom? If they believe they have and that God is the giver of this blessing, who is to say this is not true? They believe it to be so, and so it is. In a sense, they can be seen to be pardoning themselves because they believe that by fasting or confessing, they have achieved their goal.

What is tricky about beliefs and belief systems is the chicken and egg phenomenon. Which came first? Those steeped in religion or religious institutions will affirm that the belief came from God. Is it God that requires the adherent to fast or confess to be forgiven? Some who do not believe in God might wonder, is the order reversed? They would say, humans commit unsavory acts which religions label as sins. To be absolved from these acts one needs a system by which they can be forgiven. Hence the given religion contrives a modus operando whereby the offender can be released. God is invented and edicts are pronounced in God's name, and the adherent who believes in God and in the edict can then partake.

It all depends on what one believes, on the held interpretation of Truth. Hence, when something is a belief, it can be held up to scrutiny and to question, and it can be changed.

The process might have originated with the Ancient Greeks who broke belief down into three related concepts: trust/confidence, opinion/acceptance, and dogma/philosophy. It is easy to see how these concepts took hold because humans need something larger than themselves to anchor themselves in this up and down life we live. We need to trust that some things are true. We must have confidence that there is an invisible glue that secures existence so that we can function within it. We go a step further to hold opinions and accept as real those views which enable us to live in the world. Then we reach beyond our individual personalities to systems or organizations that provide religious dogma or philosophy and house it in grand physical establishments that project or seem to embody the Divine, or God.

Beliefs provide security. They give us a way to live, a way to walk through this life. They enable us to form comradeships with others who hold the same beliefs. Thus collectives emerge through which strength is provided to those who belong. Because this is true, beliefs also lead to separations since groups of people define themselves as "other," or since believers define the non-believers as other. Usually, this distinction carries pejorative overtones.

Religions divide us, but so does politics, which is equally comprised of beliefs and belief systems. We also divide ourselves by communities and lifestyles: small town *vs.* big city, acceptable behaviors and those that are frowned upon, issues of sexuality and abortion, openness or closure to immigration, etc. All of this is affected by our beliefs and whether we seek to impose them on others.

There are countries that identify themselves according to a particular belief system. In Afghanistan, for example, 99.7% of the population is Muslim. Their belief system is reflected in their customs, the prevalence of Mosques, the place in society of women, etc. They call themselves a Muslim nation.

The United States has often been called a melting pot, a grand mixture of religions, heritage, and customs. By percentages, 34% of the population is Protestant, 23% is Catholic, and 21% of the population is unaffiliated with organized forms of religion. This makes the U.S. eclectic, and yet in current times there is a vocal group in the nation proclaiming that the United States is a Christian country.

Furthermore, they believe that the U.S. was founded by Christians. Their belief is so strong that they ignore the fact that the nation was first settled by deists or theistic rationalists who believed God existed and created the universe and gave humans the ability to reason. They rejected notions of divine revelation and the Bible. They also rejected the notion of the Trinity and other religious "mysteries" which they called incomprehensible notions. They looked upon those who wore the cloth and ran religious institutions as people who sought to dominate the masses by creating dogma, rituals, and practices. They rejected suppressive religious systems. Our founders came here for religious freedom.

For followers of Jesus to call the U.S. a Christian nation because of their staunch belief is a negation of the founders' quest. Moreover, there are dangerous implications in this belief that seeks to impose itself on the entire U.S. population. It can lead to discriminating against non-Christians. It can demand that our laws line up with Christian beliefs (we already see this in relation to abortion and birth control, and school curriculum.) It can lead to white Christian nationalism and possible violence against non-believers.

In our nation's history, many beliefs have been detrimental to groups outside-the-line. Indigenous people and Black people were believed to be inferior, lesser, a thorn in the side of white culture. We know the ramifications of this: stolen lands, broken promises, government mistreatment, slavery, segregation, alienation, denial of basic human rights, withheld opportunities in business, schooling, housing, job-seeking, loans, etc. All this stemmed from beliefs and combined with power-grabbing and greed to produce lasting inequity.

Amazingly to me, until as late as April 1968, when Martin Luther King Jr. was assassinated, only five newspapers in the whole of the United States agreed to carry a comic strip that contained Black characters. That summer Charles M. Schulz introduced Franklin and showed him meeting with Charlie Brown on the beach. At that time, beaches in the U.S. were segregated. (1968!) Franklin and Charlie then went to the movies together. This was revolutionary because movie theatres were also segregated. All this was because of a belief that it was unacceptable and unhealthy for whites and Blacks to live together. Blacks were deemed inferior, unworthy, probably dirty and needed to be kept in their place, so the belief went. I am astonished when I think of this. I was 29 years old and this separative belief was solidly in place in the nation in which I lived, the land of the free!

A long time ago, a significant number of people believed the world was flat. They didn't know (key word) any better. If that belief had persisted, explorers might never have ventured forth and earthlings would have stayed in place, never exploring further lest they fall off the edge of the world and into outer space.

The Transition to Knowing

Major change is coming with the transformation. From belief to knowing. Now is the time to prepare for that shift. No matter what beliefs we hold, or what systems of belief we support, it is vital that we awaken to the fact that belief does not necessarily equate to knowledge. Many people have already begun to change, to actively question beliefs that have guided us. In the transformation we will shift from the Piscean Age to the Aquarian Age (the key words are "to know.") Beliefs will be challenged in new ways and humanity will begin to wiggle out of the clothing of opinions and ideas-held-dear because the attire will have shrunk having been washed in the light of wisdom revealed. Humans will begin to drop any thought or doctrine that has been questionable or defended only by dogma and ritual. Humans will shift from stagnant positions to insatiable curiosity. Humans will awaken and a new bell of consciousness will toll.

In the transformation, knowing will become the new way of functioning. Whereas belief is very group oriented, knowing rests with the individual. Individuality celebrates uniqueness and discovery. Belief lumped us together with others in paying homage to what the majority held as true. Belief demanded that we fall into line, that we see only what others in authority presented to us, that we cherish certain ways of being. Knowing shatters that mold. It champions differences and invites alternate ways of seeing the world.

Knowing is born of intuition. It requires that we consult our inner selves rather than depend on gurus, teachers, ministers, priests, elders, or leaders. Knowing awakens us to the wisdom that resides within us and waits to be tapped and embodied.

Knowing speaks to us in different ways. Some of us sense something and get goose bumps which send a chill through our bodies and beings. We come to know something that is unshakably true. There is never any question about this knowing. It just is. Some of us hear a big booming voice inside ourselves. It offers wisdom or direction or admonition. It is heard only by the individual but is so loud as to be unmistakable. It stops us in our tracks and forces us to see something new. It offers insight. It shifts old perspectives.

The more we listen to that inner voice, the more it speaks to us. And the more we follow through on what that inner voice says or asks of us, the more we will be given by way of wisdom revealed.

My inner knowing has helped me with all manner of things, from avoiding accidents, to finding parking spots, to being led in a career direction, to originating programs that serve personal growth, to friendships I would never have thought possible, to talents I never knew I had.

Intuition is constantly alive and ready for us to turn toward. It calls to us through gut feelings when we least expect it. It encourages us to be sensitive to ourselves, to what we are ready to tell and teach ourselves at each moment. Intuition reminds us of wisdom we have forgotten because daily life has cluttered our observing.

We were each born with intuition alive and thriving. As infants we are attuned to life pulsing around us. We can hear inside our own bodies and merge with our new world each time we touch something. We see and we know, but we have no language to communicate what we are experiencing. If we are not encouraged to sustain and heighten this intuition, our knowing begins to fade, and we must wait for a period in our lives when we can reawaken what we know.

I heard a story about a small boy who went into his newborn brother's room to ask him what the face of God looked like. He knew the infant would know because he had so recently come through the process of creation. He wanted to ask him while the image was still visible because he also knew that the babe would forget before long, getting lost in the sensory stimuli surrounding him. He himself had forgotten and he longed to know. The infant had no words to be able to tell him. But in his lighted face, his toothless open smile, his joyful involuntary movements, perhaps he was able to communicate an answer for his brother.

In childhood we have a sense of wonder. Everything around us is filled with beauty, as if everything is a miracle. We are free from the analytical and relate to life through the heart center. We are not burdened with beliefs, not laden with information. We are free spirits discovering our world and bringing the whole of ourselves to it. When we shift to knowing we will regain this interconnectedness with the wonder of life.

Knowing exists in seed life in the form of DNA. A seed automatically knows what plant it will become, how to develop, how to carry out all the chemical reactions and biological processes it needs to become what it is meant to be, and how to stay alive. Animals have knowing but theirs is instinctive. They know what to do and how to do it, but they don't know that they know. Humans have helpful DNA and instincts, but we go a step further. We know something and we know that we know. This element, this knowing that we know, is what will replace belief. And because we know that we know, we will be empowered to touch what is already in place in the universe and to give it form in reality.

When Knowing Opens a New Life Path

Knowing is easy to come by because we tune in to what is and always has been. We humans don't invent new things. Instead, what we do is wake up to what is there and register it. Once we do that, we can see it clearly and "bring it into being." It is as if we are alone one minute and in the next, we turn around and say, "There you are!" We didn't know what we were looking for, but by expanding past ourselves and the life moment, we opened and met what awaited us.

This happened in a life-changing way for me in 1971. I was living in New York, finishing my MFA in theatre directing, conducting The Love Project, and serving as Chairperson of the Speech and Theatre Department at Thomas Jefferson High School. I had taken up painting as a hobby, but I could never really get into recreating reality on a canvas.

One day I felt an urge, an inner calling, to allow the brushes to move themselves with colors that seemed to ask to be chosen. It was easy, and I enjoyed being in the flow of creativity without thinking or imposing anything on the canvas. When I finished the first painting, I noticed what seemed like a hint of a face. It was prominent in the center of the work and had an almost skeletal shape. I noted it but I didn't go to my head to try and figure out how it got there or who it was.

I continued painting in this same fashion until I had completed five canvases. To my surprise the face that had initially appeared reoccurred and became more prominent from painting to painting without any influence from me, or manipulation, or even focus. I was, however, curious.

Kendra, the costume designer on my graduate thesis production, was a psychic. I showed her the paintings and asked if she had any sense of what the face that had appeared meant. She did indeed. She told me this was someone I had yet to meet, but it was someone I loved and that we would work together. I was intrigued, and open. But I couldn't really focus on what Kendra had registered because I barely had time to breathe given the schedule I was on.

On top of everything else, my husband and I were preparing to make a major move to San Diego, CA where we planned to relocate. I had been invited there by Herb Otto of the National Center for the Exploration of Human Potential and given a scholarship to train as a group facilitator. From November 1970 when I received The Love Principles through the fall of 1971, it was as if I was on a ride that originated within and took me along from one life station to another.

In August of that year, I finished the last painting in the series, on the lawn outside our new apartment, in the sunshine by the ocean. When I looked at the finished work, I saw a full-blown face. A kind, beautiful face of a woman, probably in her 30's, with blond hair. I liked seeing her but did not connect the face with what Kendra had told me. I was simply glad to have finished the series.

On the first day of the training at the National Center, I was sitting on a tabletop when an older woman entered the crowded room. The booming voice of knowing in me told me to jump off the table, go to her, and invite her to see my paintings. By this time in my life, I listened to my inner voice without hesitation and, as I said earlier, the more I listened to it, the more it spoke to me.

Patricia said, "Yes, of course. I would love to see your paintings." As she viewed them later in the week, she said, "My friend Diane needs to see these." I immediately said, "Do you mean Diane Kennedy Pike?" as if there were only one Diane in the world. Patricia was astounded and asked how I knew that. I had no idea. The exchange did not take place in my head but rather in my heart and I simply gave it voice as I heard the question within me.

I didn't know that Patricia knew Pike, who was the widow of Bishop James A. Pike. A year or so earlier, my spiritual mentor, Ev, had sent me an excerpt from Pike's book "Search" about how the bishop died in the desert in Israel when the two of them were there on a quest in 1969. What had struck me at the time was that Diane Pike had talked to the rocks she had clung to as she made her way out of the wilderness to find help for her husband. I too knew about communicating with rocks, with all of life, because I had had an awakening experience in which I merged with everything that was.

I hadn't thought about the article or Diane Pike since, but my inner self had clearly not forgotten, and it was that voice that asked Patricia if this was the friend to whom she referred.

Way led to way. Patricia asked Diane to come to San Diego to see the paintings. Diane had zero interest in seeing someone's spiritual paintings, having been inundated by psychics who reported visions of where Jim was lost, but told Patricia, whom she thought of as her spiritual cross-over person, that she would go when she was next in San Diego. She felt safe in promising that because she had been to San Diego only twice in her life and had no plans to return.

The very next week Diane's editor at Doubleday called to ask if she would go to San Diego to address the West Coast salesmen. Diane laughed, knowing that she was really being sent there to see some woman's spiritual paintings.

The last Sunday in September 1971, Diane and I met at the Hotel Del Coronado. I was sitting in the lobby and could sense her presence when she arrived. It was one of those experiences of "There you are!" I leapt from the sofa and spun around to meet her. I instantly knew I loved this person. And that we had something to do together.

When I took Diane on a tour of the paintings, she didn't see the face in any of them until the last one, but she did know immediately that she was the face. I also knew she was the face in my paintings but neither of us wanted to be presumptuous, so we did not acknowledge the knowing. We were both amazed that she had somehow managed to be painted into my canvases, from Santa Barbara, CA to Brooklyn, NY, but it would be two weeks before we exchanged this discovery.

When she left that day, I told her we weren't finished with our exploration. When we met again two weeks later at her home in Santa Barbara, I told her we had "a work" to do together, although I had no idea what that meant. I didn't remember in that moment that Kendra had registered that same thing back in Brooklyn when she looked at the paintings.

53 years later, we still work together, grow together, laugh together, and share wisdom

with those whom we have the privilege to teach.

This is the kind of miracle that comes of opening to inner knowing. It is to be guided by a force focused on the more that is ready to come into being. Listening within with willingness is an important key as is functioning from the heart rather than seeking to control with the mind. Being in the here/now, in the power of the moment, allows the more to unfold. Being conscious and present allows us to be met by what already is and what is to be. It is important to remember to breathe, to receive, to welcome, to bring the whole self to embrace what is emerging.

There are many ways to practice opening to knowing: be mindful, be aware, meditate, quiet the self, express gratitude for each moment, breathe in and out through the heart center. If chanting serves you, you might like to use the heart chakra chant "So Hum" and allow yourself to be carried on its frequency, repeating the chant several times with rising and lowering pitch.

Listen to your body. It will tell you what you need to do and how you need to be. Listen in your heart. Listen. You will know what is right for you. Pay attention. Do what you tell yourself.

If you do listen and then don't do what your inner voice says, you will not benefit from what is being offered to you.

I recently sat in a very cold theatre on a cruise ship waiting for the show to begin. My inner voice, through my body, spoke to me loudly. "Go get a jacket." I was too lazy. I sat freezing throughout the show. Within one day I had a severe sinus infection and cough that lasted five weeks. Next time I will listen!

Knowing to Serve the Whole

The transition from belief to knowing will evoke a momentous change in how individuals live and how/what they contribute to the world. Imagine millions of people, awakening their heart chakras, and daily asking their inner selves what new, what more, what gift might I bring forth from myself to enrich life and propel us all toward our next evolutionary step?

This practice will shift the moral compass of humanity. We will move from a limiting analytical focus and from an orientation of belief to a level of empowerment few have known.

Now is the time to start moving from belief to knowing. For some people, it might feel easier to cling to old ways of being, to feel secure in beliefs and allow "authorities" to make decisions for them and to tell them what paths to walk. Others will want to continue to engage in power struggles and seek to dominate for their own ego gratification. Still others will be afraid to take a new step into the unknown.

All these people and their old age perspectives and ways of being will eventually fall away because what supports their way of life will fall away. There will be no need for their choices of belief because knowing will have replaced them. Those who cling to belief will be like relics of the past: the horse and buggy, the dial-up telephone, the foxtrot, saddle shoes, the ice box. When the new comes into being, the old shrivels and dies. In this case the new will dominate with Light and those with a lesser focus will need to protect their eyes.

When the transformation occurs and the population of awakened beings surges, they will send forth such abundance of heart center love that anything lesser will have no chance of surviving in the finer frequency that will become prevalent.

When I was a child, Hitler dominated the world. He had a loud voice and shouted his way to power. He methodically blamed the woes of the German people on scapegoats. He intended to make Germany great again by eliminating the culprits he identified and created. He stormed across Europe and over nation after nation until the Allied Forces joined together to save the world.

Hitler rose to power not only because he was charismatic but because throngs of Germans believed his rhetoric and supported him so that they could save their own skins. They stood by and watched as Jews were harassed, beaten, and finally loaded on trains bound for the final solution. Hitler was powerful because those who were looking out for themselves and were willing to benefit from acts of horror, gave him their allegiance. Without thousands following him, blindly or in self-protection, Hitler would have been left shouting to the wind: a blustering, red-faced dictator alone on a dais spreading lies and seeking to evoke violence. If no one had listened, if no one had joined, his rants would have been lost in the very air where they landed.

There are those among us today who rant, who rave, who blame, who lie, who spew hate and promise revenge to any who would defy them. Alas, there are millions who champion these hate mongers because they "believe" what they hear. In the coming transformation, this reality will change. Multitudes will turn from belief to inner knowing. They will open their heart centers, reject divisiveness, and send love forth into the world.

The numbers of those who surround the planet with love will grow exponentially. As our evolution progresses, higher consciousness will prevail and when the balance is tipped in that direction, the quality of inner knowing will be refined to the point that we will register only finer frequencies that perfectly match the highest good we can manifest individually and as a world group.

This is the new that is to come. Wave upon wave of awakened people who will hold as their purpose to look within to see how to use their life force to bring goodness, kindness, and greatness into being. They will be examples for those who are slower in transitioning. The old ways of being will be ineffectual and people who cannot lift into the new reality will struggle until they are ready to adapt.

Registry of What IS

Still another phase of the transformation will come in the form of access to all that is. Until now only a handful of "geniuses" have had the ability to connect with this frequency band. This phase will reveal the ability of everyone to do anything and everything that is of the highest good and is available to the human species. It is the art of registry of what is.

Mozart began composing at age 5. How? We might say that he, and others like him, were born with that talent. There are numerous individuals who have astounding ability in one area or another, without any training.

The gifts of dance, voice, sport agility, art,

musical composition or playing of instruments, scientific or mathematical genius, artistry in cuisine production, poetry, theatrical production, language fluency, etc., all exist in the energy world. They are there, present, always. They are available to anyone at any time. They are there for those who can move beyond the thought-world of limitation and can register, receive, and bring to life the frequency band in which the gift resides.

In simple terms what this means is that anyone can sit down at a canvas, for example, and begin to draw and paint magnificently because they have touched the frequency of the ability to do this. Or they can enter a basketball court and make basket after basket from any location. Or they can speak in a foreign language or write poetry because they have created no block between themselves and the ability.

I had a small but profound experience of this decades ago. I was in my late thirties and had just begun to learn to play the piano. I had no previous experience and couldn't yet fully read music. I had learned the notes and some chords and was practicing singing along with my playing.

One day as I was singing, I found the key was too high. Without thinking, I transposed what I was playing into a lower key. I have no idea how I did that! I knew nothing about transposing and certainly didn't have the skill needed. What happened was this. It was as if a window opened, and I could see through in utter clarity to what I needed to do to transpose the piece. It was a miraculous moment. I felt as if everything I needed to know about the piano had just opened to me. I didn't really know how I did what I did but I saw it through the "window."

Unfortunately, the next day we were leaving on a week's trip for our work. I didn't touch a piano the whole time we were gone. When I returned, the "window" had closed. My connection with the energy world of music had been severed. I was so disappointed by the experience that I gave up the lessons because of how much travel we did, leaving town practically every week. However, I never forgot the experience because I had touched into what felt like another world of possibility and capability.

I had registered transposing and could do it without knowing what I was doing. That immediately told me that the whole world of creativity was open to me if I could get out of my way.

Geniuses see, feel, touch, what is available, and they merge with it and simply do it, embody it, become it because it is there, and they "know" how to be an expression of it.

Composers of centuries ago practiced this in their earliest years and today their music is still alive and thriving. Einstein saw things beyond other scientists' imagination and his truths still influence our lives and are expanded upon.

What will this mean for individuals in the transformation that is to come? Each of us will nurture our capacity for knowing. We will see through the veils of reality to "the how" of expanding our talents, and we will make extraordinary contributions to the world. Because we will have moved from competition to cooperation, from belief to knowing, we will lift the level of creativity and productivity and bring forth inventions, creations, compositions, and abilities from our expanded potential.

Our focus on excellence will invite us to see possibilities that have been hidden from our sight but have been there all along. We will discover that nothing is new. Everything simply is and always has been. When we "invent" something, it is not that it didn't exist in the frequency world. Rather it is that it didn't yet exist in manifestation, but it is there as an essence, as a configuration of energy awaiting creation in form.

Thanks to the refinement of the quality of our inner knowing, we will register the unseen-and-as-yet-unknown because we will have lifted to the highest good we can manifest. Our coming accomplishments will go beyond anyone's wildest imaging, and we will see that the good that we have brought into being up until this point is the prelude to the great that is waiting.

From CONFLICT TO CO-EXISTENCE

In the coming transformation, as impossible as this may sound today, there will be no more wars. The frequency change will be such that war will no longer enter human minds as a thought. Killing each other will no longer be a viable concept to resolve a conflict. Thanks to the extraordinary imprint that will come to Earth from the Universe, humans will rapidly evolve to peaceful thoughts occupying their brains. This will lead to resolving tensions with a focus on harmony and inclusivity.

In the past it would have taken eons for humans to evolve to this point. This shift will be a radical change in that it will move our mental processes from warring to co-existence.

We have made extreme changes many times in the history of humankind. For example, in our earliest stages, as creatures in the sea, we did not see the color spectrum available to us today. The spectrum was always there (just as peace and co-existence have always been there) but we had not developed enough to perceive all of it.

In 2014, Emory University biologist Shozo Yokoyama and his team traced the evolutionary pathway, going back 90 million years, that led to color vision.

Among their findings was that seven genetic mutations and 5,040 possible pathways for the amino acid changes were required to bring about the evolution of human tri-color vision. "It is only when several of the changes combine in a particular order that the evolutionary pathway can be completed."

Environmental influences were not enough to drive the evolution of color vision. The change also required shifts in our ancestors' molecular environment. The researchers found that about 80 percent of the 5,040 pathways to seeing color had stopped in the middle because a protein had finally been rendered useless by a new mutation that preceded it in the pathway. "The remaining 20 percent of the pathways remained possible pathways, but our ancestors used only one." Yokoyama and his team identified the needed path that opened the way to the unlimited color we see today.

I use this example because our fixation on war and conflict might be due to a blockage in our path to peaceful living. That path will now be wide open to us. We will no longer be hampered in our access to vistas that lift humanity to union, to unity, to peaceful co-existence. It will not take millions of years for the change to occur because we have already emerged from lesser expressions going back to our becoming Homo sapiens 200,000 to 300,000 years ago.

We laboriously evolved from hominids who themselves had diverged from other primates nearly 4 million years ago in eastern and southern Africa. They adapted to living on the ground and walking upright instead of climbing and living in trees. A million years ago we Homo sapiens began to migrate out of Africa and into Eurasia where we started making advances beyond tool-making to controlling fire. Yes, it took ages for us to make that journey and to evolve into who we are today. We are by no means finished. Our minds need cleansing and polishing because we still don't see past ancient negative ways of seeking to resolve disputes.

The Universe is opening the pathway that has been closed to us all this time and soon, we will have 100% color vision of how to live together so that all of us excel and we create a new Eden in which everyone and everything can flower.

Facilitating Co-Existence

The Love Principles *Problems are Opportunities* and *Provide Others with Opportunities to Give* can help us in today's world to facilitate the process of finding ways to live together peacefully. Now is the time to begin practicing these principles to prepare for the major shift that is coming.

Today, our current tendency as nations in the face of conflict is to confront, to threaten, to warn, to activate weapons, and if infringed upon, to immediately retaliate. It is a macho response to danger, and it often is met by a macho response from the offending side. Humans immediately gear up to fight, resolve the problem with force, and supposedly be done with it.

When we live in the time of transformation, we will move beyond these limited ways of dealing with discord. We will recognize that a problem is that which interferes with the status quo. It gets in the way of how life was progressing. It demands attention. It stops us in relation to what we were doing. It is static in our lives.

Our first inclination in relation to a problem has been to solve it, or to rid ourselves of it, or to block it. It was a bother and if it was a threat between nations, it could have been a matter of life and death.

We knew we needed to address problems and deal with them. How we did that played a crucial role in what eventuated. In the new frequency, we will move to an enlightened way to deal with a problem by embracing it and exploring its gift. The problem has come to stop us from a given way of functioning in order that we might grow and expand our horizons. Problems are opportunities.

We will not have thoughts of war lurking in our heads. When problems arise between nations, they will be immediately addressed by those who are agitated and those who appear to be the cause. Instead of escalating antagonisms, leaders will ask what has caused this to occur. What are we doing that might have provoked this? Instead of immediately gearing up for resistance, we will ask the offended why they are so disturbed. We will provide "the other" with the opportunity to give us the information we need to work the issue out together.

In today's world such actions might seem absurd. What nation has ever asked such questions? Nations will do this when the shift occurs.

When the injured party raises an issue of concern, the grievance will be brought out into the open and both parties will calmly address it. The opportunity will be to find an accord together, to remedy an untenable situation. We will remember that when there is an issue there is always more than one side to the story. The opportunity will be to open that issue to the light of co-existence. We will lay the issues side-by-side. This is where the transformation will take us: to that light of co-existence.

In a world transformed, fighting will not occur. Discussion will have taken place, and that outdated stage will not be an option. Once the two sides can hear each other, can listen to one another, they will find a way to live together in peace. The opportunity is for both sides to lift higher than the specific roadblock and examine the conditions that created the problem in the first place.

After the transformation, rather than engaging on a battlefield, questions will be asked. Nations will be willing to lift the conversation to explore what new to bring into being. What are they willing to give rather than take from one another?

Each will provide the other with insights into the issues that divide them, and each will stretch to see what their nation can do or give to alleviate the concern, to make life better.

Peace Among Nations

Peace Among Individuals

Nations might emulate couples who have long, successful marriages. If they have a conflict, they don't go to sleep without reconciling their differences. Nations will take up this practice by remaining at the peace table until there is a negotiation, a reconciliation, an agreement to lift each other so that each can thrive. Nations will do this, and no one will ever again die on a battlefield.

Years ago, following the death of their mother, Diane and her four siblings divided up the family belongings. The process went along easily. First, each had the opportunity to retrieve what they had originally gifted to their parents, and then they each selected items they would like as remembrance.

But then, a serious problem arose. What to do with their mother's silver service? Diane and her brother Den were the only two who did not have silver sets, and both wanted to have their mother's collection. Neither would budge on the issue, for a variety of reasons.

Brother Scott, the youngest of the bunch who had devoted his life to peacemaking, got up and locked the door of the bedroom where the negotiations were taking place. He said that no one could leave the room until the issue was resolved to everyone's satisfaction. And so, the back and forth began.

After quite a long time, and because it was required that they come to equitable terms, the siblings finally decided. (No one wanted to spend the rest of their lives in that bedroom!) They chose to divide up the silver with each sibling getting a major serving piece and each getting three table settings. It was the age-old story of everyone getting something and no one getting everything they wanted. Coming to a peaceful conclusion was the focus and they managed to achieve it.

The transformation in human consciousness that is coming will eliminate wars. This is not such a grandiose statement. Individuals can find their way there, as can nations. One follows the other as nations are comprised of individuals.

In our current consciousness, there are active elements that have led to war. There are those who still want what others have and try to obtain that in any way possible. There are nations that want to defend their sovereignty while at the same time denying it to others because that would be threatening to them. There are those who want to fight, to dominate. There are those who seek to eliminate others or other nations because that would be expedient for them. All these, and more, threads of an old expression of human nature will become remnants of another time. In the transformation, the frequency of the heart chakra will prevail.

There will be an awakening that will jolt human beings into realizing how much blood has been spilled during the history of humankind. We will be shocked at how barbaric we have been, how we have resorted to means that have wrought havoc and permeated the air we breathe with the foulness of mass death. We will experience shame over the numbers of youth around the world whose lives have been snuffed out in the name of a cause and how we ameliorated our horror by labeling them heroes, by praising them for their sacrifice.

We will look at our human history and lament that while wars ended in peace, warring had never really ended, as we repeatedly waved our flags and marched off to battlefields.

We will dismantle all weapons of mass destruction and lift the veil of fear that hangs over all our lives. We will do away with the military. We will have cadres of people committed to the service of the whole instead.

There will be such power in this transformation that those who try to remain embroiled in issues and daily minutia will begin to fizzle. They will be out-of-sync with the emerging reality. Their former calls for war will sound to everyone like a worn-down battery, muffled, garbled. Thoughts of war will have become archaic.

We will look at what we have been doing and we will change.

We will do all of this because we will have awakened, and that will be the spur to enable rapid change of human behavior. Instead of seeking to be the victor in any quest, we will pour our energy into establishing a continuous climate of co-existence. This will facilitate the healing of poverty and starvation across the globe because everything is interconnected.

Peaceful co-existence will eliminate economic and social inequalities, and marginalization will be eliminated, such as gender discrimination, caste systems, or diminishment because of race or tribal affiliation. Instead, all people will be valued as important cells in the One Being. They will have access to the same resources as everyone else and will contribute to the whole with their unique gifts. Everyone will have a voice in how their daily life unfolds and they will be part of the decision-making process that affects their existence.

People will be blessed with good nutrition because food needs will be met, thanks to healing climate warming so there will be fewer floods and less drought. There will be no civil or global wars to halt the transport of needed grain and fruits and vegetables. Proper nourishment will lead to healthier parents and children. Children who are no longer hungry will excel in their studies and achieve successes that were never possible.

Peaceful co-existence creates a positive domino effect.

The abomination of food waste will disappear. No longer will one third of the global food supply be thrown away. Everything that is manifested will be used to benefit the whole.

Because there will be no colonial rule of nations as we have had in our human history, there will be no plundering of natural resources and a new level of thriving will emerge in one population after another.

There will be a resurgence of clean water, improved sanitary conditions, and an abundance of clinics providing needed health care.

Public servants will take pride in literally serving the people of their community. There will be government support around the world for excellent infrastructure, transportation, safety, education, and health care facilities. This will be possible because no financial resources will be poured into munitions or protection against other nations.

There will be job creation and the welcoming of all levels of talent and participation.

The millions who will have switched from belief to knowing will lead the way. By the power of their heart center love expressions, gardens of flowers will replace battlefields. They will blossom with possibilities for positive exchanges.

Heart Center Love Leads Us to Light

Peace will predominate because all of us will receive wisdom from knowing and we will function from the heart center. This is not wishful thinking but rather the result of moving from density and intransigence to the finer energy of love flow. We will have committed to the process of lifting from pedestrian to Divine.

This process has occurred multiple times from individual to individual with the result of shifting from darkness to light. There are many factors at work enabling the shift to take place.

I remember when my aged mother Rose entered a state of severe unrest. She was confused about where she was. She was distressed. She was angry. It was as if a dark cloud had formed all around her and she was trapped. I knew that this behavior could have emerged from something she feared. We sometimes respond to fear by lashing out. We roar outside at what eats at us from within. It is akin to having a beast inside that we can't seem to tame.

To reach my mother, I shifted in myself to compassionate empathy. I entered her unrest and breathed deeply. I could feel what she was feeling. Tears came to my eyes because I was sad that my mother suffered this. I was now equally affected by the unrest. It was as if she had a fractured consciousness and couldn't find her way between the two selves that were fighting to prevail.

I began to observe myself in the suffering and from a center of finer frequency I asked, "what is wanted of me?" This was an invitation to find a way to move the energy into a new expression. I entered that transitioning process within myself, sent forth a refreshed energy flow from my heart center, and mirrored that shift for Rose. Directed heart center energy is powerful. It brings about change.

Rose was drawn out of the darkness and into the new flow of heart center energy. The tone and temperature of the circumstance shifted and changed. Harmony and peace emerged. The two of us breathed and rested in the new that had emerged.

The process of changing an energy configuration from density to clarity, from darkness to light, involves consciousness, breathing, and directing life force with intention, lifting in knowing, and entering the heart chakra. In this case, my mother and I were able to become one energy field. Through my empathy I could awaken her experience in myself and stand in it with her. She was caught in the chaos and didn't even know she was. From the midst of the turmoil, I could consciously lift, on the breath, to the next level. Holding that intention, I could move myself from solar plexus to heart center, and because we had become one field, she was brought along to the irresistible finer frequency. I saw her face change as the energy shifted, first in me and then in her. It was akin to watching a miracle happen. The very air in the room changed.

This process will be achieved with larger groups of people, and with nations. It will start with one person. We have world examples of this: Gandhi, Martin Luther King Jr, Nelson Mandela, Mother Theresa. They had visions. They embodied change. They committed to their life mission. They dwelt in heart center energy, in unconditional love, and change opened before them. They set a new frequency in motion and thousands of people stood in that frequency and sent forth heart center love. They attracted thousands more. The frequency of love brought multitudes along and change occurred in the whole of society.

Until now that change stood alongside the holdouts who fought to retain the status quo. This was the case because we, as humanity, were still focused on polarities and separation. Ignorance still prevailed. Too many still were unaware that we are all One Being.

I am eager for the transformation if only because it is wearying to live in the current polarity structure where divisiveness reigns. I see it as such a waste of our talents and our accumulated knowledge. It is as if we are dressed in armor, sitting atop mighty steeds, jostling with each other to have our points of view succeed.

From Division to Do No Harm

I don't know when the transformation will occur or how long it will take for it to be in place, but I do know there is much we can do right now to stretch ourselves to meet the new reality.

We can practice creating harmony even though it is often not easy in our current situation. We can begin by talking with "adversaries," by listening to each other, by wanting to move beyond the stalemates that predominate.

I live in a retirement community. When Diane and I moved in five years ago, we were subtly informed that no one here talks about politics, or for that matter, controversial issues. The rationale for this was that we all live in the same place, and we need to get along. So, it is better to refrain from issues that might lead to ill-feelings.

This policy made me uncomfortable because it seemed to be an unnatural way to live. How would we grow together if we never went beyond talking about the weather, or our physical conditions as seniors, or focusing only on niceties. Little by little, we have met others who are willing to explore more serious issues and that has been rewarding and it requires an effort to seek out these others.

I raised the issue with our CEO. He agreed that as adults we should be able to talk about all subjects and issues. He announced this at the next resident association meeting and went further, encouraging us to engage with each other in meaningful ways. He reminded us to be kind in our discussions. If a resident did not want to engage in the conversation, that choice should be honored. I was grateful for his opening the door to our enriching one another through our different perspectives.

Some issues are easier to practice exploring than others. But we must make the effort to bring our conflicting views into the light so that we don't harbor them in darkness that separates.

From HAPHAZARD TO PURPOSEFUL LIVING

Once we are living in the new paradigm, we will all be asked to step up into greater consciousness. There will be no excuse for lack of awareness, for allowing life to simply happen to us without our taking responsibility for everything we do, or for drifting through our days without making each moment meaningful. Instead, we will welcome the finer frequencies by becoming active partners with the new reality as it is emerging.

Each of us will tap into our inner knowing and follow the inspiration that calls to us. We will proceed with decisiveness. We will direct our energy from the core of ourselves and make our contribution to the whole by living purposeful lives.

Adopting a Life Purpose

To live a meaningful life, we will need to know our life purpose. We will choose that life purpose; it will not be "assigned" to us.

A purpose is not a goal. A life purpose is like a large umbrella you hold over the whole of your existence. It is a guiding force. It needs to be large enough to serve us in all aspects of our life. It is essential that we identify that life purpose so that we can direct our energy.

At every stage of our lives, having a life purpose makes every day significant. Without it, we are aimless rather than focused. We pass the days rather than live them. If we are in the latter decades of our lives and living without a life purpose, we start to fade because we have ceased to meaningfully engage with each moment.

While it is perfectly fine to die when the time comes, the death is best accompanied by purpose for the life that has been lived. Such a life has contributed to the whole and made a difference. This will be especially true when we are all living in the finer frequency of the transformation because we will know that we are One being, one cell in the body of the whole, and that the life purpose each of us holds contributes mightily to the more we are all becoming.

Having a life purpose will be a major component of life in the transformation. It is important, then, to begin practicing having a life purpose now. This way we will be prepared and be able to step into the new frequency.

When having a life purpose was a new idea to me, I explored the subject by looking back over my life up to that time to see what my life story was about. Where did I invest most of my time and energy? What brought me the most satisfaction? Asking these questions gave me clues to what my life purpose had been or to what I wanted it to be.

My life purpose was and is to serve the creative process. That is the big umbrella under which I have functioned. I turned everything I did into an expression of creativity. When I was nine, I used to throw a ball against the wall of my apartment building in Brooklyn. It began as practice for improving my baseball and punch ball skills.

Almost immediately, it took on much greater proportions. I developed a requirement for how high the arc of the ball coming off the wall needed to be. Then I began to count how often I could make it do exactly that. How many times in a row could I do it? It was my own personal challenge to myself. Not another soul in the world cared about that arc, but I did, and I focused on it every day. Looking back, I see that it is a perfect example of serving the creative process because I made meaning out of nothing and demanded excellence of myself.

I did this with most of my very early and then later activities: working in coloring books at my little makeshift desk, taking care to choose the hues and match them; writing poetry and finding the perfect images to convey the theme; designing lesson plans that were exciting; painting canvases that invited the viewer in; doing photography that fully captured the essence of the scene in view or that captured the soul of the subject in a portrait; fully entering the character I played onstage; directing a production so that every moment matched what the playwright had written; inventing exercises to enable participants in our workshops to grasp the wisdom that was being conveyed. All these and more were actions and activities I embodied to serve the creative process. Looking back, I can see that I have and am still fulfilling my life purpose.

Once we are living in the new paradigm, we will all be asked to step up into greater consciousness. There will be no excuse for lack of awareness, for allowing life to simply happen to us without our taking responsibility for everything we do, or for drifting through our days without making each moment meaningful. Instead, we will welcome the finer frequencies by becoming active partners with the new reality as it is emerging.

Each of us will tap into our inner knowing and follow the inspiration that calls to us. We will proceed with decisiveness. We will direct our energy from the core of ourselves and make our contribution to the whole by living purposeful lives.

Conscious Choice-Making

As we practice in preparation for the coming transformation, we will see that consciously living with a life purpose blesses us with meaning for our daily existence. When making big choices, a life purpose guides us so that the choice fits into the larger mosaic of our existence. We don't coast along but rather we direct our energy in a powerful way. Our life purpose over-arches our daily activities, our whole way of being. When we hold it in our consciousness, we can use it to harness the energy of everything we do and make each moment as vital and relevant as possible. And, we can make quicker decisions about choices we have and directions we want to take. We can ask, does this fit with my life purpose?

The important element here is the integration of goals, plans, likes and dislikes, chosen actions, relationships, and even attitudes. All of it becomes a path of conscious choice-making, rather than drifting through the day.

When the transformation occurs, all of us will focus on this process because it will flesh out the lives we are living and keep those lives from being hit-and-miss. Having a purpose will enrich the fabric of the whole and enliven every cell in the One Being. It will encourage us to do what is wanted of us, each in our own distinct expression.

When the transformation occurs, we will all be contributing consciously to the purpose of life itself and our connection to it.

From the vantage point of our individual lives, we cannot know *the purpose of life itself*. It is larger than we can grasp. It is akin to looking into the endless universe and trying to comprehend what is out there, how far it goes, and what it all means. We are awed by it and yet we are a part of it. We are each a pinpoint of the whole which expands to infinity.

We contribute to the purpose of life itself through our individuality and uniqueness, even though we do not have the capacity to see and know the great design into which we are woven. We come one step closer to that knowing by participating consciously in the continual unfolding of reality. Functioning with a life purpose allows us to direct our energy toward discovering more of our potential. Life purpose is our pathway from our pinpoint of perception to glimpsing the greater reality which is beyond our ken.

From Making Love to Being Love

There are many ways to have sex. These days some people are very casual about it. The partners don't even have to know each other's name. They meet. They are attracted to each other. They hop into bed. The activity can be highly pleasurable but meaningless.

In the other extreme, partners who are deeply committed to one another set aside an uninterrupted time to give to each other, to focus entirely on each other, to make love together. And then, there is every other kind of sexual engaging in between the extremes.

Having sex began with a focus on procreation. The giving and receiving of sperm was for the purpose of populating humanity. In many cultures, back in the day (way back in the day), it was a straightforward interaction. If pleasure came as a result, that was a bonus.

Today, sexual relations have risen to an art form thanks to the removal of guilt or shame that had been imposed by cultural values or religions, thanks to the rise in experimentation, and thanks to greater freedom to live and perform in one's body. Sexual activity surmounted the definition of who shall be with whom and became a more common way for individuals of every persuasion and gender to share self.

For most, the height of sexual engaging is arriving at a climax, a total release of self, a complete expenditure of energy and life force. It is a wonderful activity, and it is engaged in often and long into later life. As it is now practiced by many, it might be called a "manufactured" means of euphoria. It requires concentration, imagination, dexterity, energy, focus, and stick-to-itiveness to arrive at the point of satisfaction. It is a worthwhile and rewarding experience.

In many cases, it can be said that sexual activity in today's world is action for its own sake. There is attraction, awakening, desire, follow through, and consummation. A complete activity unto itself.

From Climax to Union

In the coming transformation, the act of sex will be elevated from what I have described above. Sex will have a loftier purpose. For those who are ready, it will rise from an activity of release to a time of union. Union with the other person, union in Oneness, union with all that is, union with ecstasy. This sensation, this result of sexual activity, is hard to speak of in words because it exceeds words, it goes beyond description.

To experience union is to merge with another and from there to merge with all that is. It is to move from making love to being love.

Those who are ready will be lifted into a heart-centered frequency that will be so powerful that people's relationships with each other will change in multiple ways. We will care about rather than confront each other. We will support each other rather than subjugate anyone. We will cherish rather than chastise. There will be kindness rather than condemnation.

We will be focused on how the life of everyone can be respected and revered. The emphasis in every situation will be on what contributes to the greater good combined with what avoids doing harm to anyone.

All issues confronting us will be explored on levels beyond intransigent stands, beyond religious beliefs, beyond protests, beyond arguments.

Every aspect of every issue will be explored with heart-center love and everyone, together, will determine individual solutions born of compassion for everyone involved. We will focus on the holiness of the life of everyone concerned and this will lead to making choices that serve everyone equally. We will lay all issues equally side-by-side, no longer taking sides and creating divisiveness, but making room for all possibilities so that both sides can live together in harmony.

This enormous change will be aided by humans having discovered union in daily life, and having discovered it in elevated sexual interactions that take the participants beyond self to being love, to knowing another as self.

Beyond the Sexual

For some, the transformation will bring even greater change: from making love, to being love, to union with the Whole, to living in euphoria continuously because the Crown Chakra will have opened and a merging with greater light will have occurred. I have tasted this, and it changed my life forever.

It is not easy to talk about, not even necessary to talk about, but when I do, it often evokes amazed responses. One of them provoked great humor.

Over dinner with friends one evening, I was describing my vision of transformation that is imminent. Everyone was very excited about the coming change until I mentioned that humanity would make a shift in relation to sexual activity, that the act will soon be for the purpose of union and not just for pleasure. The men at the table stopped breathing. I went on to report that I, myself, had moved beyond the sexual. There was still no breathing at the table. I said I hadn't had intercourse in 53 years, and I didn't miss it. That broke the ice, or the breathing that had been halted. It was a wonderful moment and worth sharing here.

One of the men, threw his head back, roared with laughter, and loudly repeated what he considered to be my unbelievable statement: "She hasn't had sex in 53 years, and she doesn't miss it!!" He was beside himself over the notion that one could do without sex.

His animated response of disbelief led me to expound further and cause even greater laughter. I said that the act of sex was a lot of work! It led to an exciting climax which then required several moments of pleasure-filled rest. Then, the event was over, and I would need to reinstate the process, redo it, to achieve a similar result. I said it wasn't worth the effort, especially because I had replaced the activity with something more lasting. I had moved from the temporary thrill of titillation to the ongoing experience of perpetual ecstasy.

The men at the table settled down at this point but it was evident that not many understood "perpetual ecstasy." I could see that when the transformation occurs, the change in orientation to sexual behavior, to holding a purpose of union, might require more time.

I did not arrive at my "beyond the sexual" state without having thoroughly explored and delighted in sexual activity. I did not have a desire to be a celibate individual.

My sexual awareness began as a young tween when I had an encounter with the bar on my bicycle. This led to the awareness of body parts I never knew I had. Like most teenagers, I experimented with sex, enjoying kissing and touching but drawing a line at penetration by the male because I was raised to "save" my virginity for marriage (a very outdated concept these days.)

When I got married and had intercourse, I delighted in the activity. My husband and I enjoyed a very active sex life. He was a wonderful lover and making love was a passionate experience.

And we were very aware that we were "making love," as differentiated from "being love."

When I used to engage in sexual activity, I did have the sense of lifting beyond myself, of touching heights of great excitement through thrilling stimulation. It was wonderful for me and for my partner. When we arrived at a climax together, it was as if we became one being entranced in pleasure.

I see that this was a foretelling of engaging in sex for the purpose of union.

After four years of marriage, my life completely changed. In 1968, at age 29, I experienced life-threatening heart disease. I was completely out of commission for six weeks and on limited activity for six months. Sexual engaging was out of the question. I wasn't physically able. What I didn't know at the time was that the "illness" was the beginning of the opening of my heart center (chakra.) It led to my "awakening" in 1969.

The "awakening" was a cosmic experience that so changed the makeup of my being that sexual expression became utterly lesser in my life experience. In fact, it became a downer when compared to the spiritual ecstasy I had come to know.

My spiritual awakening was a unique experience altogether. It required no effort, it lifted me into a state of joy or rapture or grace, and it never really left me.

I came to know something better than sex, something beyond physical orgasm, beyond pleasure.

To this day, over fifty years after my last experience with intercourse, I have neither missed sex, nor craved it. That act simply could never touch the state in which I live, the exquisite connection to all that is.

Because of what I have come to know and the frequency in which I live my life, I can easily say, yes, there is astounding life beyond sex.

I don't know if this step is right for everyone, but it will surely be more prevalent in the coming transformation as each of us experiences greater connection with all that is.

In the coming transformation the scales will be rebalanced in the direction of Oneness. As that happens, the whole of humanity will be drawn to the new. We will shed our limited perspectives and open to endless possibilities as we gravitate toward greater light. We will no longer need to seek love or make love. We will become love. And in that becoming we commence the journey from human to Divine.

From HUMAN Toward DIVINE

Until now we have known ourselves as human. When we have thoughts of the Divine, we have placed it in a category beyond us. We walk the earth while winged angels fly about us in other realms. We sense the Divine exists. It is where creation lives, where miracles occur, where God or the Creative Force lives.

Because we don't yet know ourselves as Divine, we brought into being a class of people known as ministers, priests, lamas, gurus, etc. to act as intermediaries who develop systems, methods, rituals, and dogma to connect us with those lighted realms. The time has come to bridge the gap and merge with the more our true selves are ready to become. The coming transformation will bridge the gap.

The true self is the cell in the Body of God. That true self is God in manifestation.

To know the world of the Divine and to transform ourselves, we must come to conscious knowledge of the Energy World. We must be able to lift from dense to finer frequency, from darkness to Light, from the material to the spiritual.

Although we think of ourselves as solid, we are in fact energy, as is everything else in manifestation. Because we think of ourselves as solid, we extend that thought or belief to the opinions we hold, to our interpretation of how life should be, and to everything else in life. This perspective reinforces the false idea that we are separate and that what we say is true, is true. Living in the material world reinforces rigidity.

Changing Forms of Energy

The fact that we are energy rather than solid is supported by Quantum Physics and Thermodynamics. The basics of these sciences fit perfectly together with what I have intuited spiritually in terms of the relationship between all forms of energy. The energy in the universe cannot be destroyed, but it can change from one form to another. This is what the coming transformation heralds: that we are about to change from one form to another.

Forms of energy include what we see as solid mass and non-solid matter like heat, light, sound, etc. Quantum physics tells us that energy is stored in mass particle form. This applies to thoughts, feelings, attitudes, beliefs, habits, customs, and rituals. They are all composed of energy.

So how is it that we experience our bodies, chairs, oranges, flowers, etc. as solid? Quantum physics tells us this happens because everything, every cell, every molecule is composed of energy that is superimposed on itself. This produces an image appearing substantive. The degree of energy that is superimposed yields the image that emerges. But all of it, everything, is really energy. It is not solid at all, not stagnant, not as it appears to be.

Beneath all the superimposition, the reality is that everything is 99.9% empty space. The sum of it is hardly enough to be thought of as solid. Everything is spinning and in constant motion.

A ceiling fan can easily depict the difference for us. When the electricity is off, we see the blades as solid, each one separate and unto itself. Yet, when we turn on the fan, especially to its highest speed, we cannot see the blades at all. We can see right through the spinning to the ceiling.

Here is another example of how we appear to be solid even as we are constantly moving bands of energy. On the campus where I live, an amateur astronomer has set up a powerful telescope in a small observatory so the residents can view the activity in the sky. Seeing Saturn and its rings through the telescope was an unforgettable experience for many of us.

Recently we have been invited to view clusters in the universe, but rather than see them through the eye of the actual telescope, we sit in a room and view the pictures sent by the telescope to TV screens. I reported that this viewing is not nearly as exciting as looking through the eye of the telescope where I feel I have a more intimate experience with what is being viewed. I was told that the reason we have to view such clusters on screens is that they are much further away and if we looked through the telescope, we would see only blurry little spots.

What we see on the TV screens is a composite of pictures of the magnified spots, a stacked view of them, one magnification on top of another bringing us closer to them and resulting in a form that we can recognize.

This is like the process I spoke of earlier of molecules superimposed on molecules until a clear image appears. At first the cluster seems like fuzz in the distance. Then one image is stacked on top of another and the energy seen in the telescope solidifies into a form that we can see through the magnification in the finished image on the television screen.

If we explore from this other direction, from the cluster we can now see, and peel back the layers, we can go back through the visible views, to the essence, to the energy.

We are not what we appear to be and are

instead superimposed dynamic energy composed of consciousness and constant vibration.

If we apply all this information to the beliefs we hold dear, we can only laugh at the importance we attribute to them since they are basically empty space.

Consciously Moving Energy

When we shift from belief to knowing, we enter the energy world and touch the vital life force that is ever flowing through us. What we register is a constantly moving vibration that pulses. It is connected to the force that creates life itself.

When Diane Pike and I began our work together in 1972, part of our focus was on channeling healing energy through our hands. We have been practicing the technique for many decades now on our own bodies and on others in need of healing. The results have been rewarding and in line with the knowing that everything is energy. Here are some examples of healings that occurred over the years.

We moved energy in the sinus area to relieve a cold, pulling it out to the sides of the head till the pressure was relieved.

We moved energy up and away from the head and forehead to quell a headache.

The two of us stood, one at the head and one at the feet of Diane's father when he almost fainted and was not fully connected with his body. We channeled energy until we felt him stabilize and he was able to sit, stand and walk with balance.

When we bang a leg into a piece of furniture, we start the process of moving the energy immediately and watch as the blood ceases to rush to the top of the skin. We work until there is no "black and blue" mark.

When arthritis flares up in a joint, moving the energy removes the inflammation and allows the cells to come to a place of rest.

A more dramatic example occurred one morning as I was cutting a bagel. The sharp blade of the knife slipped and cut deeply into the fatty part of my hand along side my thumb. Blood began to pour out into the sink. Diane rubbed her hands together to activate the energy. Then, holding her hand about 2 inches above the wound, she began to move it over the gash from the wrist out through the fingers. She worked for about ten minutes. During that time, I watched as the bleeding stopped and the gash began to close. When she finished, I had a single line scar, as if I had had stitches which were removed a while ago and only the line was left.

When practicing moving energy, our hands always remain above the body rather than on it. In this way, the process is energy to energy.

In the 1970's and 1980's, there were healers in South America who performed what I would call "energy surgeries." For example, if a person had an obstruction in her stomach, the healer would enter the area and heal the condition. He did not make an incision with a knife. Instead, he turned the solidness of his hand to light, to energy, and moved directly into the body, through the flesh (which also turned to light and energy,) and the repair was made. It sounds bizarre and unbelievable, but it was more like a miracle for the one who was healed.

Quantum Physics explains the energy world as waves and particles. Each wave holds the potential for what the particle will become. When we connect with inner knowing, we are entering the wave of potential. That potential is in constant motion. To see what is emerging we must enter a field of clarity where there are no expectations. We want to touch the finest frequency possible. When we do this, we lift beyond the material world and touch the Divine.

New Ways of Thinking

As we approach the coming transformation, science is exploding with new information. This is because collectively we are ready to allow new thought to penetrate our consciousness. The so-called new thought has always been there, but we have not been ready to meet it or merge with it. When we refer to the evolutionary process, we are really talking about something that is, and always has been, something to which we are now awakening. We evolve to meet the more that is. This is the energy in the universe that changes from one form to another.

Science is now exploring how DNA can be influenced and reprogrammed by words and frequencies. This field of study is vast, but it affirms the wisdom of Indigenous groups who used chanting to bring about change, to hold the earth in balance, to effect healing, to lift consciousness. They were in touch with the energy world and the power therein.

On a visit to a Tibetan Monastery near Lhasa, I could feel the power of the chanting of the monks. The atmosphere in the room changed as the chants progressed. The frequency of sound and its effect was palpable.

Scientists previously dismissed about 97% of DNA only to discover that what they referred to as "junk" contains codes that would lift us into finer frequency functioning. This would directly correspond to the transformation that is coming in consciousness.

Scientists are working with coding beyond the level of molecular DNA. They are exploring the combination of consciousness and the environment which tells us that we are a vibratory organism that can use thoughts and word structures to establish higher levels of self-organization. This points to our next level of evolution, or our next level of merging with what is and always has been.

For decades, Diane and I have practiced "reprograming" ourselves through sound and words. We had no idea that we might be changing our DNA, but we could certainly feel how the frequency of sound affected both healing and changes in personality.

We have practiced and taught toning, a system of using sound to move energy and to lift our frequency. When we began a group session, we would tone an elevating Ah sound. This would reverberate throughout the room, draw our focus in from the road from which we had arrived to centeredness within the group. It would quickly establish a group field and support our purpose for being there.

We would also use toning for healing ourselves and others. We would tone the person's given name so they could feel themselves coming into realignment. If we had discomfort or pain in our bodies, we would use toning to move the energy. We would start with a tone well below the place of the pain and move the sound up the scale until we came to the blockage. Then we would repeat the sound focusing on the physical site until we could feel the energy shift. Soon a stream of clarity would move through the blockage, and we could affirm the change that had occurred.

This is sound frequency vibration in action, positively affecting the living organism.

When I talked to the cancer cells in my breast, I was consciously using words and the images they conveyed to instruct the cells as to how they could go to sleep so as not to suffer pain when they were cut from the body. This was not wishful thinking. It was direct communication to the living cells. It was a purposeful action from a conscious being and real results eventuated.

In the beginning was the word. The word was obviously a wave that was filled with potential from which life was born.

The Next Wave of Potential

We are all affected by the movement of the planets through outer space. Astrologers have talked about this for ages. There are torsion waves which are carriers of consciousness. The torsion wave energy in the universe affects both the planet and every living being on it.

We are entering a time of higher concentration of that energy during this shift to the

Aquarian Age of Knowing. This intensified concentration is what will encourage the evolutionary process on which we are about to embark. It will spin us beyond our accumulated knowledge and refine the quality of our intuition. It will contribute to moving us to our new level of being.

All of this speaks of what is coming in consciousness for humanity in the transformation. It affirms expansion beyond old beliefs and movement toward Universal Wisdom. There is no doubt this is where we are heading. Paradoxically, a confirmation of this shows up in today's polar expressions of rampant resistance to change.

Officials are banning what they call "Woke" because it exposes truths that threaten white society and calls it to task for its wicked past.

Super Right bloggers are calling for local Christian churches to "run their towns." Their fear is great that non-believers will replace the Christian doctrine and Jesus will lose his stature as savior (even though he never really fulfilled that promise of being the Prince of Peace, given continued wars over the last 2000 years.)

Politicians and world leaders are frantic to control the narrative of how things are to be, and they do it through any means possible: lying, obstructing, prohibiting, and belittling.

This thrust of resistance is a last-ditch effort to control. They desperately want to keep their tower of power from crumbling.

But Universal Truth cannot be quelled. It exists beyond boundaries, and it is the next wave. It contains the potential to shift the whole of humanity toward a Divine level of functioning in which anything lesser will not be able to survive because it will burn up in the Light.

The shift into the Divine will be a celebration of our ascent into finer frequencies in which our higher good will shine more and more every day. Those who persist in shouting, grabbing, and clinging to the old order will lose their grip on reality. They will no longer be supported by the new gravity born of the increased vibration from the planetary spheres and they will tumble into their own depravity and be forced to adapt.

Our current world struggles with good vs evil, but once the transformation takes hold, we will embrace all that is good in each of us, and we will move forward to lift ourselves beyond good to great, to living in the Light.

From GOOD *vs* EVIL To LIVING in the LIGHT

Good *vs* Evil, as I said earlier, has been the human struggle for a few millennia. While good seems preferred, in fact devoutly to be wished, very little is said about it. If you look "good" up in Wikipedia and contrast it with the discussion of evil, you will find pages and pages of dissertations and philosophy on evil but little about good.

If you read newspapers or watch the news on television, you are not often exposed to many stories about people "doing good." The news will have about 90% of its focus on terrible things that have happened and on problems and catastrophes. It would seem we humans have a fixation on what is bad and what is wrong, rather than on what is good.

I once read that good deeds are not considered to be newsworthy. Headlines about terrorist attacks, crime, murders, and malicious behavior are what sells. As a people, we seem to be magnetically drawn to what we want to eliminate in our own lives. That others are doing dastardly acts is a perverse fascination of ours. We say about the evil deeds, "That is terrible!" But we are transfixed, nonetheless.

Good as an adjective means something to be desired or approved of. As a noun it is that which is morally right, or it is a benefit or advantage to someone.

Good represents preferred conduct when given a choice between possible actions, and it is the opposite of evil which is undesirable. It is basically angels vs the devil.

Good has to do with ethics, morality, religion. If we go back more than twenty-five hundred years to when the good vs evil quest began in ancient Persia, a religious philosopher called Zoroaster spoke of two opposing forces that were in constant conflict: one illuminated Wisdom, the other destructive spirit. In our western world, this idea developed into religion which shunned the material world and embraced the spiritual. Gnostic ideas influenced ancient religions with praise for enlightenment, salvation, and oneness with God.

As time went on, good was thought of as that which should prevail and evil as what should be defeated. After all, good is life-affirming and just. It is affiliated with happiness and love. Evil is associated with deliberate wrong-doing, harming, humiliating, destruction and often leads to violence.

In terms of morality, evil is incorrect behavior causing pain and suffering, filling the world with negativity. It is the opposite of good or even the absence of good. It is wickedness. Religions such as Christianity think of it as demonic or supernatural. Evil is to be feared and avoided. It is an ominous force.

Hindus see evil's roots in strife and suffering. Their philosophy focuses on bad actions rather than bad people. There is a balance of good and evil and when that is disrupted, divine incarnations are needed to restore balance.

In Buddhist thought both good and evil are part of an antagonistic duality that can be overcome by achieving Nirvana. Desire is the root of evil, as is illusion. Both cause suffering. The primary duality in Buddhist thought is between suffering and enlightenment.

In Confucianism the primary concern is with correct social relationships with behavior appropriate to the learned individual. Evil is wrong behavior.

In Taoism evil is the opposite of compassion and humility.

Islam is different in that it believes that everything, including what is perceived as good or bad, comes from God for our free will to choose.

In Judaism, evil relates to free will. Humans must choose the path of goodness in the face of temptation. The virtue is in the choosing.

Philosopher Baruch Spinoza saw good as useful to humans while evil hinders us. If the human mind has adequate ideas "...it would form no notion of evil."

Carl Jung depicted evil as the dark side of God. Thomas Aquinas defines evil as the absence of good.

Most human beings are good, or at least try to be. But we don't seem to elevate ourselves beyond the goal of being good, useful, a benefit to others, or if we hold to a given religion, morally correct in our behavior. If we avoid evil, we think we have achieved the goal Zoroaster set in motion. We are not destructive spirits. But Zoroaster spoke of good as embodying illuminated Wisdom. This is what is coming in the transformation, and once we make it, we will not only be reflections of illuminated Wisdom, but we will move, as humans, into greatness, living in the Light.

From Good to Great

Over many decades, segments of the population have experimented with drugs of various kinds to touch expanded consciousness. LSD was a favorite, producing euphoria, out-of-the-body experiences, spectacular illusions, and a sense of power. Those in the altered state thought, while under the influence of the drug, they could accomplish anything.

Having had a natural awakening of expanded consciousness I didn't need a drug to produce it. I live in a recurrent euphoria. Bernini captured what I experienced in his sculpture the Ecstasy of Saint Teresa.

Gian Lorenzo Bernini's sculpture capturing the Ecstasy of St Teresa. It is in the Cappella Cornaro in Rome.

In my awakening I experienced who I was beyond the body and even came to know that I was not my body. Moreover, I was not *in* my body, rather my body was *in me.* I knew that I could create all manner of wondrous things and that I had no limitations. I didn't need spectacular visions because when I looked into ordinary life, I saw it in vibrant color and knew that it was not solid, but energy in movement. This is important knowing for moving from good to great.

When the transformation occurs, the nature of life as we know it will change. We will no longer live in polarities of positive vs negative. We will shift to good as a baseline and great as a new and pervasive human expression. The highest good will summon us and because of the shift in frequency, that will be all that will call us.

The frequency of the planet will change so that only that which is filled with the glory of creation will reach us, nothing less. And we who are good will drop from our consciousness anything that stands in the way of that, anything that pulls us toward the lesser or denser, and we will be filled with light. We will be made light so that we can shine love in the world. We will become co-creators with the Divine Forces.

To become great, the composition of our bodies, our minds, our very beings, will change. As we once shed our ape-like configuration, so we will shed the density we resort to whenever something troublesome appears.

We will greet adversity with tones and actions that shift and change reality. And we will watch with awe as the new, the fresh, and the clear becomes what appears substantive and alters the molecules so a new, joyful expression comes into being.

I know. It sounds amazing. It is unfathomable. And to think, all of us will be making this shift and thus humanity itself will become completely other than what it is now. And the process will not be disturbed by those desperately clinging to the old ways because they will not be able to survive in the new frequency.

The old order will dissolve like ice cubes in a glass of water, and they will merge with the new or eventually evaporate. Evil will no longer be expressed. There will be no more focus on causing harm or on destruction. That soap opera will be cancelled by the Network. And morality issues will shift and fall away because belief will fade and be replaced by inner knowing.

I see it coming. I sense myself being lifted. I can imagine what this world will be like when everyone is devoted to love, to serving, to creating wonders, to being kind and generous, to merging with the Divine.

Will this happen to each of us at once, like a shifting of earth's plates in a monumental quake, or over time as is the style of evolution? If it happens all at once it will be as if all of humanity hears a high pitch sound that is no longer hidden from us. We will feel the rising of life force within that moves our awareness up the inner tree of life into the realm of the Crown Chakra and beyond the top of the head. We will feel ourselves being lifted, being stretched. We will feel ourselves being called and we will embrace the sound, the new frequency.

If the new occurs all at once, the momentum for this change will be in full gear. There will be no stopping the transformation that is coming to those of us grounded on earth. Many of us are right now moving toward a new reality. There is work we need to do as we prepare for this. Each of us needs to look at our lives to see what to release and what to enhance. I can use myself as an example.

Eradicating Useless Patterns

Moving toward the new reality involves letting go of ways of being that jam me up and cause frustration. These old expressions have me repeating behavior that has not served me and keeps me locked like a hamster on a wheel. I recognize that I need to step off, examine what hampers me, and do something very different.

Turning to the wisdom I have gained; I created a checklist of obstacles I and others seem to repeat ad nauseum. For example, I remind myself that I am better off when I am not immersed in feelings that churn. It is important to feel, but turning those feelings over and over as if turning milk to cream keeps me from moving forward.

I listen to myself lamenting about something going on in the world. I repeatedly comment about how awful it is. By speaking this way, I begin to feel awful. A scowl takes over my face. I am bogged down in the awfulness. It is a useless pattern. To get out of it I need to breathe, to move the energy, to create a new reality. I need to be the change I want to see happen so that I can begin to feel hope.

Another pattern, in which I get stuck is to invest energy in opposition to opinions of others that rile me. It is really none of my business what others think. There is no reason for me to see their views as a hinderance to me and how I live my life. I hear myself saying, "How can they think that way? What is wrong with them?" I am creating displeasure in myself over what they hold as an opinion, and I am the one who ends up being unhappy. How ridiculous is that? I can shift to focus on my own opinion and to make sure it serves me in creative ways.

Worse still, I have a pattern of overwhelming myself with my own fierce opinions. They are strong and immovable. I become chained to my own righteousness. I want others to think what I think. Seeing how entrenched I can become I don't even think it is healthy for me to think what I think. I am a prisoner of my own mind. It is ok to hold convictions but not to have them hold me. I can practice sitting loose to what I think so that I can change when it is necessary.

Often, I activate a pattern of intolerance of behavior of others that offends my sense of morality. I didn't even know I had a strong sense of morality. But obviously I do because when other people do things that do not meet my standards of what is right and wrong, I create outrage and get off on a tear about their behavior. To continue doing this is senseless because others are going to do what they do whether I like it or not. It would be better for me to look at my own moral convictions and live them. Period.

I often get caught in politics. I need to stay out of it altogether, support who represents policies I consider good, and refrain from side-taking. Right now, we live in the world of polarities of so-called good and bad. Those who represent the "other political party" are all too frequently seen by me as the opposition. They are really the balance to what I hold to be true. I can break this pattern by remembering, every day, that we are all One. That we bring differing points of view to every issue and that we can start to lay those side-by-side to come to a new wholeness that represents all of us and takes us forward.

A pattern that is strong in me is the resistance I create when others commit acts that hurt children. I feel the pain of that deeply in my solar plexus. I can hardly stand it. I value that I suffer because of these actions by others. I know that the suffering goes nowhere and doesn't change anything. Yet, I persist. This torture of myself needs to be eradicated and replaced by daily expressions of love for children. And I need to bring heart center love to those who hurt children so that they might dissolve some of the anger they create because of the forgiveness and compassion coming toward them.

Then there are the things I label as an injustice, and all the causes to which I rally. Yes, there are injustices and yes there are multiple causes for me to support but I need to temper my responses and my involvement if they become so consuming that they create imbalance in my life and interfere with my bringing good into being.

I see myself as good because I tell myself that these stances represent decency. They are appropriate behavior for a good person.

Many of us are committed to these expressions of good because of the passion we arouse. We put our whole selves into everything we feel, and we feel good about it! But this pattern is not an expression of greatness.

Greatness would be lifting above expressions of good. Remembering that what disturbs us is fleeting and that the more of our energy we invest in agitation, the more we enter our personal on-going soap opera. It is a soap opera in which we have played starring roles. Good is not the act of becoming someone who rescues people from their suffering. Good is to stay out of the trap of thinking we can save the world through our expressions of good.

Great is to take that a step further, to stand

as a light of unconditional love that embraces the whole and lifts it up to union with finer frequencies. To function in each moment as if angels are right there to help transform the moment.

Great is becoming a co-creator. It comes from listening to what is calling to us from within. We are currently at the wonderful stage where we hear wisdom and look for ways to embody it. Because we are good, we use wisdom to create positive realities. Now we are ready for the next and even more profound level.

Letting Go of What Has Been

While we haven't yet looked in the face of the transformation, we are all experiencing the dissolving of what has been. It is happening before our eyes. The earth is hurting. It is loudly communicating with us through global warming, radical shifts in temperature, storms, extraordinary rainfall and floods, earthquakes, high tides, erosion, melting ice caps and glaciers, and erupting volcanoes. It tells us to wake up and change our ways of living immediately.

Collectively we are not responding fast enough. Those who control leadership on the planet are still more focused on the economy than the ecosystem. The goals set for the needed earth changes are too far in the future. We think we are in charge, in control, but we are gravely mistaken. The consciousness of earth itself is greater than the actions of the human inhabitants. Earth will do what she needs to do for herself.

The earth is calling to its guardian, the Universe, and it is reshaping the energy world of our planet. It is raising the frequency. It will no longer allow the existence of the forces that threaten earth's health and existence. The finer frequency will dislodge everything that tries to get in the way. I have an image that as the earth tilts differently toward the new finer frequency, those humans who don't move into the new balance will fall off into their own chaos.

I hope that all of us will lift ourselves to yield to the shift. If we don't, many in earth's population will die. While I would like to see this avoided, I am also aware that humans are dispensable. We are inflated with self-importance but when viewed from the perspective of the whole, and beyond that, of the Universe, we are not vital to the Cosmos.

I am reminded of Genesis and the tale of Noah's Ark (mythical or based on the stories of the great flood in Mesopotamia.) Perhaps we are being called by the Creative Force to the Ark of Consciousness so that we might not only survive but thrive and facilitate the emergence of Greatness and repopulate the globe.

I hope there are multitudes who are sensing what I see coming and that they will rise to embrace the Earth, to acknowledge Oneness, and to mirror the new for those who perpetuate destruction. Those who are in denial about climate change, who live in separation, will be mired in their own creation of sludge, too dense to survive the Light.

I have read that scientists and physicists see that the Universe is sending waves of healing energy to earth to retain the planet's stability. The Universe is the earth's support system.

We know the whole is greater than the sum of its parts. The planet is greater than the earthlings who inhabit it. Seen from the great unknown, our self-importance is reduced to barely visible specks. We need to get over ourselves lest we be over (and done.) This is not a threat. It is the truth of what might happen if we don't leave behind the reality of good *vs* evil.

The earth is at its tipping point. It is speaking to us through its own metaphors. Its tears are the melting glaciers. Its flooding is a desperate cry, a continuous sobbing. Its quakes are trying to shake and wake us. Its fires are its rage. Its erupting volcanoes are its upheaval of disgust. Its tornadoes are its bellowing warning. Its crop destruction and famine are starving us. We will wake up or we will be permanently put to sleep by the suffocation of our own world pollution. Or perhaps we will quicken the whole process and eliminate ourselves with our weapons of mass destruction. What a shame that would be.

But we don't need to destroy ourselves. We can integrate Oneness, Consciousness, and Greatness. If we choose to respect and embrace each other, the animal kingdom, plant life, and life itself, we can become the new that is just beyond us.

In the coming transformation, the planet itself will evolve, shifting under the influence of altered movement in the Universe. It will breathe in a new way and expand from the inside out. This will affect all living things: plants, animals, humans, oceans, and the very air that brings the breath of life. The transformation is unstoppable, and it is good. Evil will not be irradicated. It will simply have no chance. We will no longer be in the Age of belief or struggle. We will have moved to greatness and Light will reign supreme.

PREPARATION

The transformation in consciousness is coming. Whereas we don't know when or how long the process will be, we can prepare ourselves so that we will be ready to make the shift and greet the new. The main point in the preparation is to function with consciousness and make choices that lead us from good to great. Our preparation will also help to facilitate the transformation itself because we will be actively making way for the finer frequency that is coming. The image I see is akin to waves coming to a vast shoreline and thousands of people moving across the beach in a stream of joy to meet and merge with it.

Our overall preparatory focus should be on making "good" the standard of every day and easing our way into "great." Each of us needs to determine how much of our time and energy we want to put into this endeavor.

As I look at how to prepare, I will make this focus of good something I do not only every day but throughout the day. I will raise my total standard of living by making choices that align with the finer frequency I sense just beyond the veil of this, our current existence.

Here are some of the many things I practice to help me prepare for the change that is coming. Some of these I have already done for a long time. They have worked for me, and I will now intensify my focus on them to see how much further they can take me. I invite you to choose from among these suggestions, to add your own, and to eliminate what doesn't speak to you.

Wake with Gratitude Every Morning

When I wake from sleep each day, when I open my eyes, I express gratitude for being alive, for having yet another day in which to grow. I am grateful for the unknown that lies ahead, and for the opportunities to be an example of love and kindness.

I give thanks for all that has preceded this day, for my awareness and consciousness, and for my ability to sit up, to stand up, to enter the day.

There was a time in my life when I was limited in my ability physically. When I suffered heart disease in 1968, the life force available to me was minimal. It was hard for me to breathe, and I had no strength to do the simplest things. I couldn't lift a comb to run it through my hair. I had no appetite and could barely eat. I had no energy to worry if I would live or die. I was on my back for six weeks.

I remember the day I sat up, got up, and could take a few steps on my own. I learned about gratitude that day. Gratitude for the smallest movement of my legs, for the breaths I was able to take, for the few morsels I was able to eat and enjoy. I had never known such gladness before. I immediately saw serious illness as a teacher, as a blessing so that I could appreciate life. Before this time, I just lived life. I hadn't thought to be thankful for it. Heart disease at age 29 was a great gift to me.

Each of us can benefit from contrasting experiences in our lives so that we can more fully learn about the importance of expressing appreciation for what we have and for what is.

My first trip to India was a life-changing experience, and I was merely witnessing poverty, not living it. I looked out my hotel window in the early morning and watched as families on the street corner gathered up their sleeping rolls and their meager possessions and left them by the lamp post as they headed out to work. Work that was surely strenuous labor where each earned $1 for the day. No one touched their belongings because everyone recognized that sidewalk and lamp post as their home.

I headed for the shower where soft towels awaited me and I wondered how far they had to walk, and what they ate. Where did they wash?

In Varanasi people used the side of the hill along the Ganges River for their toilet. Then they all bathed and worshipped in that same river, and they filled their small brass jars with the same water. They considered the Ganges water holy and took it away with them.

On that first trip I was in India for six weeks. A few in the group we led wanted to leave, to go home. They couldn't stand witnessing the poverty, the filth, the overcrowded conditions, the overwhelming hubbub of the cars and their horns, all merging on broken roadways with cows, chickens, donkeys, elephants, pedicabs, and endless people.

I was glad to have the six weeks. It gave me time to lift above the living conditions I witnessed and to be touched by the people of India who were living in those conditions. Maybe, if they were lucky, they had a single change of garments. So different from my bulging suitcase.

The people had so little. They lived on the street or in shacks with rusted tin roofing, or in humble huts. And yet, each person was filled with love. When they walked past me in the alleyways, they were fully present, offering a greeting of Namaste (which means "I honor the divine in you") from the full of their hearts. They had little that was tangible, but they were alive and filled with gratitude and they were ready to do anything for me, seeking nothing in return.

The people in India shared freely of themselves from their souls when they encountered others. I was touched to my core by the beauty that radiated from the people. Gratitude was not for things; it was for life. And life to them was clearly a worship, every day. I couldn't help but think of hotel bellmen in the states who are gracious and helpful in delivering bags and then stand waiting for a tip!

In the West people walk past me and never see me, let alone look into my eyes. I am a stranger to them. There were no strangers among the poor in India. Everyone was a gift from the gods. People treasured each other and I was filled by each of them every day. And every day, I returned the gift. Gratitude was lifted to new levels for me as I had the privilege to leave western culture behind for a time.

Gratitude emanates from the heart center. If I were to create an animation of it, I would portray my chest expanding, pulsing forth with continuous energy that reaches far and wide, as well as opening my capacity for thanksgiving. I envision myself with a bowed head, in utter reverence, with tears upon my cheeks, standing in holy appreciation. The more gratitude I put forth, the more

I am filled with energy to give. It is a wonderful phenomenon.

When I feel gratitude surging in me, I feel larger than myself, filled with joy. I feel capable of more because I am thankful for what I have been able to give. That sense of feeling unlimited capacity to give is a component of moving from good to great. This is what I want to amplify as I get ready for the transformation.

Call to Praise Someone, to Express Thanks

Speaking of gratitude, another way we can prepare ourselves for the more-we-will-become is to call someone in our life for whom we are grateful and tell them so. It can be someone you engaged with just yesterday. Someone who touched you and made you feel glad. A call the next day is an affirmation of the loving exchange you shared. It is like a thank you note only delivered by voice. It is to stretch the blessing into the next day and thus make it twice as meaningful.

Think of all the people who have brought something good to your life over the years. No doubt you thanked them at the time but imagine what it would be for them (and you) if you reconnected with them today because they still hold a place of meaning in your life.

If you are lucky, you can track down the person who is hopefully still alive and able to receive the blessing you are about to bestow.

In 1982 I looked for and found the phone number for Mr. Latner. In 1954 he had been the teacher of a typing class I was required to take. Twenty-eight years later I reached him. His wife answered and I introduced myself as one of his former students. When he got on the line, I told him my name (as it had been) and was about to tell him why I was calling when he interrupted me and said, “I remember you, Arleen.” I was astonished.

I took a breath and told him I was calling to thank him for his fine teaching and to express my appreciation. He had given me a skill that served me as I worked my way through college as a temp through a typing service. Because of this, his class was one of the most important I had ever taken.

I told him how I still remembered to sit up straight (I am still doing it now as I work at my computer.) And it was in his class that I first experienced that I could train my hands to do something automatically. I could type without needing to look at the keys. (I don’t remember how he taught us to do that, but it was astonishing to me.)

When I finished offering my praise, Mr. Latner told me I had made his day. “No,” he said. “You have made my whole teaching career worthwhile.”

My call to him was an act of goodness, but the impact on him moved it a notch toward greatness. I had brought joy to someone who wasn't expecting it. I had given him an affirmation that he had made enormous contributions to the lives of those he instructed. He was enriched in the receiving and I in the giving. Acts such as this help to encircle the past and present with love.

Praise is an energizer, and it encourages goodness to flow in the world. I offer it several times a day when interacting with others. If I am making a reservation on the phone or calling a help line, I listen for what is praise-worthy and I never hesitate to offer feedback. I express gratitude for the patience of the one on the line, or for their speaking slowly and clearly so I can easily understand them, or for how well they have learned English as a second language. They are always grateful in return for my saluting the way they do their jobs. These are offerings of goodwill, and they serve to reinforce excellent treatment for the next caller.

Whenever I am in a women's rest room, if the person doing the cleanup is present, I always look her in the eye and thank her for keeping the facility clean and well stocked. Every time I do this, my offering is received with gladness. It is my way of saying, "You are important. You make a difference."

This practice of offering praise imprints

the whole energy world even as it is offered to a single person. It creates an environment of recognition and deep satisfaction. It lifts everyone involved in the process and it touches the greater field of life itself which is positively affected as a result.

Offering praise celebrates life and the simplest of offerings. If we are thankful for an action by another and we think it but don't speak it, we are being good and we are, even in our silence, lifting the frequency of the world around us. But if we take the time to speak the praise, to offer the gift to another person, we are filling the world with the sound of acknowledgment, and it is as if we are creating a love song. When we do this, when we voice praise aloud, we move from good to great because we are embracing another human being and honoring their value. In doing so, we elevate their value. This elevates us all.

Focus on Something Beautiful in Nature Every Day

Connecting with the natural world is nourishing to the soul. Our days flit by in hurry with tasks that require our attention. Before we know it, dusk is descending and the day is ending. We have spent our energy on accomplishment and necessity. That is fine, but if we have not given ourselves an interlude with nature, we are more like automatons than living beings.

The natural world is sustenance for us. It is filled with life that is pulsating in harmony, rich in color and texture, and ever ready to awaken our senses. It invites us to connect with what is organic and it bathes us with beauty. To evolve from good to great, we need a dose of nature every day so that its beauty can awaken pleasure in our busy lives.

When the mundane dominates and we are knee-deep in our agenda, we bypass awe that waits to speak to and through us.

If you have a watch that can ding you at an odd time of the day, let it be a reminder to get up, stretch, breathe, and go outside to commune with something green. Allow yourself to have a sip of thriving life.

It is not enough to glance at some trees or a group of flowers. Take the time to stand against the bark and experience its age, its journey, its throbbing. Smell a plant or flower and allow your mood to be shifted by the fragrance. Touch a leaf or petal and bring your gentleness to meet its velvety texture. Stay long enough to know that this palate of vibrant colors adds depth to your day's moments and encourages variety of expression in you.

Stay a few more moments until you are fully aware that you are never alone and that you are never disconnected from the grand life force that surrounds you.

If you remain inside the office, the kitchen, the factory, or the garage, know that you are inside your head where thoughts dominate and rule your day. You have separated yourself from the book of life and you have become nothing more than a memo devoid of joy but devoted to data.

Connecting with beauty changes your frequency. You can feel the difference. You can feel yourself being lifted and shifted.

To merge with the natural world is to infuse yourself with sensation. To expose yourself to beauty is to awaken you to possibility. It makes you smile and opens you to wonder. How could Mother Nature possibly have conceived of such a variety of color, shape, sound, texture, and subtlety?

Each creature has a touch of uniqueness. No bird species is like any other and there are more than 10,000 of them! The Mother has created a yellow beak here, a web foot there, feathers that flutter, feathers that flare, stripes and solids, a squawk here/a song there/a chirp/a whistle/a coo/a hoot.

Get out in it. Be reminded of uniqueness and difference and know that you are never limited or boxed in to any one way of functioning.

Bring your personal beauty to merge with the beauty of nature. Enrich yourself and be expanded.

Remind yourself every day, "I am more than I think I am. I too am created by the Great Mother. I am rich in color, alive with senses. I yield to the passing breeze. I am not rigid. I pulsate with life. I am growing and becoming new every minute as is the natural world around me."

There is never any need to sink into trouble or worry if you open to something of beauty in nature. It will remind you to lift, to touch life's potential. Beauty has a way of melting our hard edges, of allowing us to hear a sweet song. It brings tears to our eyes and touches our hearts.

A day without merging with beauty is a day of separation.

To prepare for the transformation we cannot afford separation. We are One with all that is, and it is for us to acknowledge that throughout every day. Communing with nature, drinking a cup of beauty, coming toward life with an open-heart center is stepping forward to acknowledge, "I Am."

Make Verbalizations Meaningful

There is power in what we say because

those words imprint the whole of the environment in which we live and everyone around us. When we carefully choose what we have to offer, we have clearly listened within for inspiration and then configured phrases that carry substance. This enrichment invites those present to listen with acuity and to lift themselves in spirit as they awaken their own creativity.

Some people start to speak, hold the spotlight, and never stop unless they are pointedly interrupted. If permitted, they could go on and on and on even if the people to whom they are speaking nod off or leave the room. I have experienced this, and I can hardly bear to be in their presence, even if I care for them.

Other people do the opposite. They rarely speak, don't have the courage to interject, think what they have to say is not worthy of saying, or they don't feel competent to express their ideas.

Those who reflect before they speak, speak purposefully. Usually, they make their contribution and fall into silence. What is good about this practice is that their words linger in the air giving listeners an opportunity to absorb what was offered.

When we choose the words we speak, we eliminate excess. And when we do that there is power in what we say, and we make a meaningful contribution.

Here is a sample scene to communicate what I am advocating.

She: "I don't feel good about your being here. I don't know why but I wish you would leave. I'm very nervous about even saying this to you."

Alternative, devoid of excess:

She: "Leave!"

In the strength of that single word, a command is issued, and her desire is fully expressed. The way she put it the first time was wishy-washy, overly explanatory, and never really said what she wanted to communicate.

When she said "Leave," it carried strength and got right to the point. That single word utterance was an example of The Love Principle *Create Your Own Reality Consciously.* She knew what she was feeling but he didn't have to know that. What she wanted to communicate was that she didn't want him there. She wanted him to leave. A single word, spoken with authority and forcefulness, created a reality that pointedly delivered her desire. He will, of course, make his own choice about how to respond but that is not the issue.

It is for each of us to be concise, succinct, and to function with clarity. This moves us along toward our highest and best, toward greatness.

When we communicate in this way, without excess, we say what we mean, and we mean what we say. This doesn't preclude our speaking at length if we have more to say; we can even be lyrical or poetic if we wish. It is rambling that represents the distraction.

Excess clutters and lessens the import. Great painters put on their canvas only what is necessary by way of strokes and color to communicate the theme. Anything more confuses or takes away from the power of the piece. This is true with oral communication as well. We attempt to "paint" an impression with words. To do this, we breathe into what we sense, we touch into knowing, we select the words that are representative of our offering, and we speak them with consciously directed energy.

None of this interferes with the flow of the conversation. Rather, it makes it more dynamic. It eliminates cliches and repetition. It needs no preface, no explanation. It creates a direct line with those who are present and everyone is stimulated and enriched.

Years ago, I delivered a talk to a large audience at a California church. I was, in fact, in the middle of talking about the principle *Create Your Own Reality Consciously.*

There was a full pitcher of water on the podium. As I stood to the side it, I used my arms to gesticulate. I knocked over the entire pitcher which did not fall but dumped all its water on the stage in front of me. The audience was aghast. I took a breath and looked for what to say.

I needed a succinct statement to move us beyond this moment. I didn't want to appear embarrassed, to excessively apologize, or to create further disturbance. I searched for the reality I wanted to create in that moment. I quickly reminded myself I was in a church.

I stepped forward and said with great enthusiasm, "Watch me walk on water!" It took only a split second for those present to catch the joke, relate it to the story of Jesus, and note that I gave them an example of creating a reality there and then. The whole auditorium erupted in laughter and then applause.

Listen to yourself as you speak and edit what you say as you say it. Find the words that best express what you wish to communicate. Listen within for inspiration. Bring forth words as a gift and wait until they are unwrapped, received, and responded to, before going on. This practice makes encounters more meaningful. The words add to the growth of everyone present. They move us from chatter to dialog, from good to great.

In the coming transformation, words will have greater power than ever before. The words will carry energy frequency and as they are spoken, the reality they seek to convey will become manifest. If someone says, "I love you," the whole environment surrounding those present will be filled with the power of love, the energy of the heart center. Everyone will immediately feel a shift toward tenderness and warmth; smiles will emerge on faces because of the power those three words will convey.

Whatever we say will impact everything and everyone around us. If someone tells a lie or belittles another, all those in attendance will register the energy those words represent, and the effect will be instantly tangible. The lie will create a crawling sensation inside our skin and discomfort will reign. The derogatory words spoken to another person will cause us physical pain and a souring facial expression. Such hurtful words will create a sick feeling in those who hear them.

Lesser expressions will become completely unacceptable because their negative impact will be immediately manifested, and they will be seen as disharmonious to the whole.

In the transformation, when and as each of us aligns with the finest of frequencies, what we utter will take an energy shape that we will see and feel as an image appearing substantive. This will certainly change the way we speak because we will be responsible for what emerges in full view of everyone. If we create something darker, denser, or disharmonious, it will not survive in the presence of the predominant Light.

This will be an extraordinary shift and it will require that we all maintain higher consciousness when we speak or act. Thus, it is important to begin practicing now, saying what we mean, and doing what enhances the whole.

Do Something You Never Did Before

To prepare for the transformation and be ready to step into an unfamiliar frequency, do something you never did before. Ride a horse, scale a wall, eat something you never tasted, walk blindfolded, shoot an arrow, milk a cow, play a tuba, jump on a trampoline, write a poem, sing an aria, make a casserole, mount a soapbox in a public place and deliver a message, brush your teeth with your opposite hand, take an ice-cold shower, belly dance, etc.

The coming transformation is something none of us have ever experienced before. We will be stepping into unknown territory, touching a reality that has not existed, and we will be called into a level of consciousness that might be overwhelming. This is a good reason to prepare by doing things we have never done, going places we have never been, saying things we have never said.

When entering a new realm, it is imperative that we *Have No Expectations, but rather Abundant Expectancy.* This Love Principle will serve us very well as we enter the unknown.

We cannot anticipate what is coming. When we are in it, we will not compare it to what we have already known because that is a step backwards. The new cannot and should not be grounded in prior understanding. Hence, *have no expectations.*

We can practice this now by remaining wide open to what is occurring and how it makes us feel. Where does it lead us? What does it ask of us? Meet the unknown fully and yield to the wave of energy it represents.

Create no limitations in yourself in relation to what is transpiring. But do embody *abundant expectancy.* Come with eagerness, with wonder, with awe. Sit on the edge of your life, because, in fact, you are on an edge, ready to soar into the more.

We can prepare for this by doing something every day that is different from the routine that holds us in our comfort zone.

One of the best practices for living in the moment is to purposely shake up the status quo. It can be accomplished in simple conversation if you say something you were thinking but would never say aloud. I know a couple whose wife dominates every visit. He can barely get a word in even when she encourages him to relate a story. He begins; then she jumps in and finishes it. I often want to say, "Please, let him speak." I usually refrain from doing that for all the reasons we all know. It's impolite. It's none of my business. It could upset the woman. It could end the friendship. Etc. Etc.

But what if I did jump in and say what I would never say? I truly have no idea what would happen. It might be that she is unaware that she dominates every conversation. Or, he might find his spine and agree, "Yes, let me speak!" Feelings might flow instead of words. It might be the beginning of a whole new stage of their relationship, and ours. Who knows? And that's the point, we don't know. Interceding like that might lead to a breakthrough long overdue.

Purposely shaking up the status quo might occur if I choose, throughout the week, foods I have never eaten or foods I have rejected or foods I have never liked. This would force me to meet head-on something strange or previously distasteful. I would have to open myself and receive and be present without any resistance.

This could also be accomplished by listening to music I have long rejected because it is dissonant or too loud or abrasive or boring. It represents a frequency I have banned from my life. If I practice opening to it, I stretch myself and I expand my tolerance.

We are going to be thrust into a transformation. Readiness for that shift will be greatly enhanced by an open, awe-filled reception. This will also allow us to adapt more quickly and to integrate the new more easily. We can practice right now by trying the unfamiliar.

Begin Functioning as Your True Self

You are more than you appear. Practice saying "I am not who I think I am." You are not the personality self. You are not the character you are embodying in this life play. Even though you have starred in this role for many years, it is time you recognized that you are more than the costume you wear in the world.

You are the consciousness that creates the personality who walks about daily. When you know this, you can choose who to be and how to be. And you can do this at any moment. You can choose new expressions of self, new qualities, new behavior. You can do this in an instant when you know yourself to be the creator.

You can practice this every morning when you get out of bed. For example, you can choose to be nimble, eager, and filled with enthusiasm and see what that does to your body, your emotional life, and your thoughts. How do these characteristics change your walk and change how you greet the day? Be aware of what changes and shifts in you. You are the creator of your reality. But you cannot know that if you think you are fixed in one set of characteristics.

You are not your thoughts. You are not your feelings. You are not your body. You are not your beliefs. You are the one who chooses your thoughts, feelings, beliefs, and therefore you can change those and your entire self at will.

A most profound example of this occurred during an Act One of The Theatre of Life. A participant suffered severe back trouble for many years. She had tried a raft of healing methods, surgery, chiropractic, massage, pills, etc. Nothing really alleviated her pain or her limitations in movement.

During an experience where she created a whole new character, she put on random garments and stepped into the role of "Thor," her name for him. She fully embodied Thor and walked about the room, even danced, and leapt. As Thor she had no pain and no physical limitations. We all watched in amazement.

At the end of the experience, she returned to her own garments, leaving Thor in a small bundle on the floor in front of her. When she started to move, she was once again in pain and again experiencing all her previous limitations. It was remarkable. It was a testament to what can happen when we align with the true self and know that we are not our bodies.

The next day, participants repeated the experience. Each approached the bundle they had left on the floor, put on the garments (put on the character they had created) and allowed it to take over. Once again, Thor moved with ease and without pain.

On the third day, participants were asked to choose only one of the garments they had used to create the new character. It didn't matter what it was. It represented the new that had emerged and could now blend with the "person" the participant had played all their lives.

Nancy chose Thor's shoes and once again, her own body shifted to his and she was pain-free and flexible. It was not because of the shoes! It was because she had shifted in her consciousness and taken on a whole new way of moving in the world and interacting with it. If she could have found and aligned herself with her true self, she would have been able to move without pain, and without needing Thor. As it was, that was still a piece of work she needed to do because without Thor she reverted to the body's old way of functioning.

Another way to practice functioning as your true self is to focus on a pattern you are aware of in yourself, a pattern you don't particularly like and wish you would not bring to life. For example, perhaps you "get" easily rattled by change, even small changes in your daily routine. The truth is that you don't *get* rattled, you create upset. You can make a new choice about it.

A way to become conscious of "getting rattled" is to "play the upset" writ large. Anytime throughout the day that something interferes with your flow, consciously create upset over it. Create grouchy. Create a furrowed brow. Complain. Stomp about. Etc. Observe yourself while you are doing this so that the next time this behavior "takes over" without your being aware of it, you will be better able to sense the behavior and you can make a new choice about it. Because you have had the practice of exaggerating the upset, you can easily calm yourself and take the disruption in stride.

Practicing this, you will become very adept at *creating your reality consciously.* You will become more familiar with your true self, the one that brings that personality of yours into being every day. This is not only empowering but it will enable you to move from good to great.

Walk Heal to Toe and Lift

How we walk and move makes a difference in welcoming the new. A good practice for this is to observe your own walk and to make changes to it when necessary. Your walk is a symbolic representation of how you greet life, what you seek, and how open you are to the new.

Always walk with your head and eyes facing straight in front of you. Look at where you are going, rather than at the floor. Looking at the floor pulls your shoulders and your frame over.

Look *into* what is before you and not just *at* it. Experience the colors, the texture, the energy of it. Allow it to call you as you approach it. Listen to what it is saying. Consciously bring yourself to meet it. Practice merging with it and allow it to merge with you. Your interaction with daily life will change if you do this.

When you walk, place your heel on the ground and consciously roll your foot and heel up toward the toes. As you do this you will feel a lift in your every step. The lift will not only be in your body, but you will feel it in your internal organs and in your heart center. Your receptivity to life will expand and you will be welcomed into the air in front of you and all the promise that it holds.

As you practice this you will begin to feel yourself lifting into your head centers, the top of the crown chakra and beyond. This is what you want to lift into: the beyond. Each step will bring with you all that is in front of you with which you have merged.

This practice of lifting prepares you in the lightness of step for lifting from merely walking on the earth to opening to the possibility of flying. It is a form of levitating in place one step at a time. It reminds you constantly that you are more than who you think you are. It lifts you from ground orientation to Light. And yes, this most certainly prepares you not only for the transformation, but it also invites you to continue opening to the more, to the unexpected.

Heal Yourself

The new that is coming is an entirely different wavelength. You want to come to it whole. Now is the time to do a self-examination on all levels to heal any brokenness in self, any hurt place, any regrets, any unmet longing, or places of emotional pain.

Is there something that lingers from childhood, something unhealed, some deficiency? How can you address it now? How can you find closure? How can you be there for the self of then when others were not?

If you came from a family where no one hugged or held you as a child, have you filled that need sufficiently in your adulthood? It's not too late. Go to a loved one and ask for what you need. You may not need it for the you of now, but you can ask for it for the you of then and allow that child self to sink into the arms of this person who cares about you. Be quiet, be still, and drink the love into the child who needed it.

Do you have regrets? It is possible to heal those now? If there is something you said that you wish you hadn't and the person to whom you said it is still alive, can you reopen the moment from long ago, and say now what you wished you *had* said? Or can you say something now to bring healing to that awkward moment so long ago? Old wounds like this heal over but there is still an emotional scar.

I looked the other day to see if I had any regrets I needed to clear, and there was one, only I couldn't remedy that because the person was no longer alive. My regret was that we had broken off communication and there was no way to heal what had caused the split. To repair the regret, I reentered the last time we had communication to see if there would be a way to release that energy. I am glad I looked.

I had written a letter of feedback and because of that letter, my former high school teacher had severed all connection. She had asked me not to write again, not to be in touch. I honored that for the remainder of her life.

I am glad I reopened this chapter of my past, because reexamining it, I see that I have no regret about having written the letter of feedback. In it I spoke the truth as I knew it for me, and I see now that speaking the truth and sharing my observations is as valid for me now as it was all those years ago. I don't know, and will never know, what in my letter evoked her severing. Because I will never know, I can let go, and especially because I can validate my action back then and not regret it.

There had been other people in my life with whom there were periods of non-communication, but in every case, healing had occurred and with it came resolution. Looking back, I see that in each case, during the time of breach, I never stopped loving the individual and continued, every day, to send heart-center energy to that person. I also value this in myself as I review it today. I kept the channels open from my side and sustained the flow of love energy. Since this is what my life has been about most of these 85 years, I am glad to have this confirmation that I have fully lived one of my primary life purposes.

I encourage you to look to see if there is anything that remains unresolved, broken, painful, or the like. Then, enter whatever that is and move the energy or seek resolution if that is possible with the other or at least within self.

Years ago, my brother did something that I judged to be unforgivable. Notice I did not say that it *was* unforgivable but rather that I judged it to be so. I didn't communicate with him for a long time. One day, I looked again at what had happened, at the action that led to my severing. I had no idea if he cared about the situation but when I looked, I saw that I was withholding energy and investing it in a grudge. This was unacceptable to me because it represented a block that I was creating, and that block lived in me!

I breathed deeply and waited until I was ready to free that energy. Then I looked to see how I could do that. Eventually, I wrote my brother a letter in which I described how I felt when he did what he did and said that I no longer wanted to stifle the energy flow within myself.

Resentment is energy that is withheld and is therefore available for giving.

I told my brother I forgave him for what he did. I felt a wonderful release within myself as I posted the letter. He never responded to the letter (although over the years we have since talked occasionally) but he didn't need to. I was the one who had created the block within myself, and I had released it.

To enter the finer frequency that is coming, clarity of being is necessary. We all still have time to clear the channels and open the way to moving from good to great, to living in the Light.

Eye to Eye, Soul to Soul

Earlier I mentioned what it was like to be in India where people in the streets were fully present, looking deeply into our eyes when they passed us or greeted us. Perhaps I noticed this in them because I do it myself and it is important to me.

Every time we greet one another there is an opportunity to touch soul to soul. What this means to me is that I look into the "being" rather than the personality, into the core and depth of the person in front of me. I can merge with that being and have an experience of our Oneness.

When we don't look "in," we look past. We glance. We engage in "sweet nothings" and move on. We lightly brush as if we were shadows cast on the pavement, walking by without getting into substance.

When we move to "great," we will not whisk by each other because it would be like leaving nourishment on a table that had been set for us. We will all slow down and take time to get to know each other. We will not bypass a part of self. As a result, we will each become a great deal more than who we are as individual units. We will come to know ourselves as part of the grand mosaic of humanity and be enriched beyond measure.

As I greet a stranger, I often stop the person and ask: "What is the most meaningful thing in your life?" The person is taken off guard and pulled into my field. They sometimes ask, "What did you say?" I repeat the question. Every single time I have done this, the person zeroes in and brings forth a response. Then together we elaborate a little. A few people have even turned the tables and asked me the same question. Our exploration is brief but significant. And two will have become one as we touch each other and enrich each other.

As you practice relating to the deeper being of each person you meet, your ability to connect on this profound level will become stronger. This will ready you for the new way of engaging that will come in the new paradigm.

Love a Stranger

There are people in our lives whom we love. We know them or are related to them, or we have formed a personal relationship with them. They are our small circle of people who are closest to us.

When we make the shift to "great," this small circle will be extended to acquaintances. The next step for us will be to expand to strangers. This would mean that anyone we pass in the street could be the recipient of the same love energy we bring to those in our personal circle. Beyond that, we will extend the same love to everyone in the world, and beyond even our planet and into outer space. That is how far our love will be able to travel.

I know that is difficult to imagine now, because personal love expression is reserved for a handful of people in our lives.

How can I practice this now? First, I must know what awakens in me when I am in the presence of someone I love. I know I instantly smile. I feel warm all over. My heart center opens. Everything around me brightens. I feel joy. My eyes soften their gaze. I feel a rush of energy going from me to the other.

If I say "this just happens to me" when I am with a loved one, then I have no jurisdiction to create this series of sensations at will. I limit myself by saying the other person evoked this in me.

But if I get on the inside of this expanding sensation and watch how I create it in myself in relation to this other, I now have the power to recreate this in relation to anyone, to everyone!

I know it sounds out of the ordinary, but because I have practiced this for many years, I know that it is very possible, as well as easy to do.

While waiting my turn for an x-ray at an imaging center, I noticed a middle-aged couple sitting to my right. They each held tightly to the hands of the other. It was clear they were concerned about something. When they quietly talked to each other their love was palpable. They were deeply connected and present to each other.

Before long an intake worker came to consult with the man. I heard snatches of the instructions she gave him. Something about a scan, and injecting dye, and it would take about an hour and a half. It was certainly a bigger procedure than I was about to have for my knee.

I felt overwhelming love for the two of them. They were strangers who had just become part of my immediate family.

After my quick x-ray, they were still in the waiting room. As I passed, I stopped to speak to them. They looked up out of their love cocoon to listen to me. I looked directly into the man's eyes. I said, "I couldn't help but overhear something of the scan you are going to have. I wish you blessed results with nothing serious in the diagnosis." Both immediately responded by reaching up in their energy to meet me, to thank me. The man went further. He said, "I hope your results will be good too." I thanked him and left.

The three of us had just shared a profound

moment of love exchange. I could feel the energy of it like an expanded balloon that had enveloped us. We were no longer strangers.

[Before continuing, I want to call attention to the brevity and concise wording of my communication with the man. It is another example of making verbalization meaningful. I spoke only two sentences and those few words carried the power of the blessing and hope for his well-being. I might have weakened the communication by saying "Excuse me. Sorry to interrupt but I want to say something to you." None of that was necessary. I went directly to what I wanted to say, and it carried the power of the love energy.]

My motivation for beginning this practice of loving strangers happened early on in our work. My purpose was to profoundly touch the hundreds of people who came to hear the talks and keynote addresses that the two of us delivered across the continent when we presented The Love Principles. I wanted to communicate the value of the Principles and I wanted everyone in the audience to be surrounded and embraced by their power, and by love energy.

After the talks, when individuals came up to thank us, I continued to radiate fully from the heart center and to wrap each person in that love. It was not only genuine but continuous, as if there need never be an end to the flow.

Doing this at talks opened me to doing it anywhere, at an airport, a grocery store, a random street encounter, anywhere and with anyone. I was creating love energy, and it was the same as I would create for those closest to me. It was a reminder that we are all One Being, that there was no separation.

When the transformation comes, all of us will be able to love a stranger because no one will be a stranger. This will be evidence that we have shifted as human beings from good to great and that we are moving closer to Divine. The sun shines everywhere equally. It does not say, "I will illumine only this small patch of earth where stand those personally close to me."

Loving a stranger is part of being an active force of love in the world. One of the hallmarks of this way of being is kindness. Because human beings are currently "good," we see this expression of love all around us much of the day. People hold doors open for others. They pick things up that have fallen so someone doesn't have to bend. They offer to carry a grocery bag. They help lift a suitcase into a car trunk. Simple acts of kindness bring a flow of love to the world.

In the market recently, I called upon a taller person to help retrieve a container of milk that I knew would be too high up for me. As it turned out, the milk variety I wanted was not there. I thanked the person anyway for being willing to help. I had enough at home to last through the week, so I wasn't concerned.

A minute later, another tall woman came up to me. She had heard my request but didn't realize the milk was not up there. She saw only that I did not get the milk into my cart. She said, "Was there something you needed that I could get for you?" She was extending the kindness, thinking that the other helper had not been able to reach it. I thanked her and said I was ok, having enough milk at home.

Expanding the kindness even further, here is what might have transpired next if I really needed the milk. This second woman would have told me to stay right there while she went behind the scenes to where the supply of milk is kept. She would then ask the shelf people if that milk was available and if it was, she would bring a container of it to me. Then she would ask if there was anything else I needed that she might help me retrieve.

Being a force of love in the world is going the extra mile, extending self, going out of your way to be there for someone else. It is gratifying to do this. It fills the giver with as much gladness as the recipient. Knowing this, it is important to practice The Love Principle *Provide Others with Opportunities to Give.* When we do, we allow people to rise to the occasion, to perform a service, to practice being love. It is a gift we give to others.

Temper Side-Taking: *Be the Change*

This is one of the most important of the preparations. Imagine a house that has only sides. It could never be stable, and it cannot protect against the elements without a roof. It also needs a floor or grounding. This is true for humans as well. We cannot take sides, support one and negate the other because we will create instability. We need to put a roof on top of differences so that we begin to see that all sides are a part of the whole. Each has validity in the structure of life. The two need to live together. Without embracing all of it, we cannot make choices that serve the whole.

Side-taking is currently a predominant way of life especially in these divided times where groups of people have separated themselves from others and live in camps of righteousness. It is as if the twain shall never meet because the opposing sides are so unlike each other they will never manage to see things the same way. Nor do they want to.

Side-taking diminishes who we are and tears at the fabric of the whole. No one trusts anyone and everyone on the other side is seen as a horror, a liar, an abomination seeking to deceive.

A new approach is coming with the transformation. We can begin preparing for it now.

In the new frequency we will move beyond taking sides and place our differences side-by-side. We will seek out the nuggets of truth in each, and together, create a reality that speaks to both sides.

Trying to do this in our current way of living is a tall order. Some people simply want to drop out. They have turned off the news and they no longer listen to either side. To do this is comforting because it is to leave the fray and live in the quiet of self, letting everyone fight it out and kill each other if necessary. Let the chips fall where they may and deal with the results when the time comes.

Those of us who are activists find it impossible to shut self away. We need to hear what the other side is saying, and we need to take appropriate action.

Here is where The Love Principle *"Be the Change"* is so important. *Be the Change You Want to See Happen Instead of Trying to Change Anyone else.*

I have people in my own family who fervently believe in the "other side" of the issues. They are as unyielding and belligerent as I am. If the subject is raised, blood begins to boil and, of course, we get nowhere because neither of us can convince the other of the validity of what we are saying and neither of us can move past the assessment that the other is simply ignorant or blind or stupid beyond hope.

If the change I want to see happen is that I want the other side to change, I am stymied before I begin. But neither will I change to accept their position.

It has all gotten so bad that there seems no way out and nothing seems to work: not listening, not stepping into the other's shoes for a moment, not acknowledging that we live in a world of polarities, not even remembering that "*Problems are Opportunities*" (another of the Love Principles.)

What to do? How can I *be the change*? What change do I want to be?

I need to lift above the dilemma, above the issues, above the side-taking. What I want is to devote my life force to life-affirmation, to love, and to creativity. Can I do that? Will I do that?

I need to put all my energy into that focus. I need to discipline myself not to get caught in the words and deeds that emanate from the "other side." I would like to simply ignore them. In the real world that is not so easy. But I can catch what I label as their negative output as if it were a giant gust of ill-wind, take it in through my heart center, and therein convert it to love, to creativity, to life affirmation. That very energy that they foist on the world I can capture and rework and, like a boomerang, send it right back out as a bolt of light to shine in the darkness. This is how

I can prepare for living in the transformation.

Every single time I am enticed to take a contrary position to "right the wrong, to save the world," I can breathe into the power of my creativity, shine ever brighter, and love with even greater force. I can satisfy my own soul by sending love rather than using my life force to rile up my character/personality and send it as a warrior to the battlefield.

If I don't embroil myself in the issues, I can be a free spirit. I can contribute to life affirmation. I can be a song of hope instead of an anthem heralding a cause. I can be the change by lifting above the issues.

While all of this sounds easy, it is not. Every day another "assault" from the "other side" hits the news. This requires significant boomeranging of light, every day!! It is tiresome and not working as well as I would like.

Hearing those words, I must look to see if I have expectations that what I am doing will work, that the other will change. If I have expectations, I have created my own trap. I thought that by being a force of love the other would change.

The Love Principles all work together as if they were one sentence. I can't do one of them while not doing another. I can't be the change and have expectations about how that will change others.

Back to the drawing board. What change do I want to be?

I really do want to lift above all this daily tumult.

As an example, let's look at the issue of global warming to see how I/we can move from taking sides to laying the issues side-by-side.

Is climate change a serious threat or is it exaggerated? Is it real, asks one side. Is it made up, asks the other side. If it is real, is it human-caused by excessive burning of fossil fuels or is it a natural process given that the climate has always changed and, as some scientists say, we are emerging from a mini-ice age and therefore warming is occurring.

Some say it is not a pressing problem and renewable energy can be brought in slowly. Others view it as more urgent with a need for action and immediate change.

One side trusts the media and the threats of danger while others view the media as hyping the issue and skewing the data. Some people trust science and others don't.

Shall the government regulate industry, or does it do more harm than good? Are stricter regulations worth the cost or do they hurt jobs and the economy? Do humans have a negative impact on the Earth or are they too insignificant to have an adverse effect? Should the Earth's resources be carefully used or are there enough to use them freely? Should policy be made without considering corporate interests or should they have a primary role?

Laying these two points of view side-by-side we can say that we should not be excessively burning fossil fuels because we are influencing the environment, and we can acknowledge we may also be in a natural process of warming after a little ice age. Given these two elements, we can cooperate with what is transpiring by seeing that in either case, we can have a major role in what is transpiring. We can be more responsible so that the Earth has an easier time of making its adjustment.

This is one way of acknowledging both points of view. We can *be the change* by looking for the elements of truth in each presentation. We can look to see how we can listen to the opposite position and be open to it rather creating outrage in relation to it. We can ask each other, what are your concerns? How can we meet in the middle?

Together the two sides can look at how to cooperate with the change, be it natural or human caused. We can reduce the burning of fossil fuels but not so radically or quickly that it completely disrupts industry and livelihoods. We can eat more vegetables and less meat and produce less gas into the environment from cattle. We can recycle, compost, reuse paper bags instead of plastic, fill rain barrels, be discriminate in water use.

We can have more discussions between climate advocates and climate scientists. We can acknowledge each other's concerns and feed the contrasting viewpoints into a cooperative investigation. We can open our heart centers to each other so that we can hear each other and join forces rather than opposing the other side.

By laying the issues side-by-side, we can agree that we all want to thrive on every level, and we can look to see how everyone's input can merge so that no side feels unheard or unconsidered. Working together in this way we will arrive at cooperation and a united front on addressing the problem. In that unity there is great strength because we will have combined our concerns and our vision for the future.

We can temper side-taking by consciously directing our energy and by responding rather than reacting. In this way we would all lift above the fray. We would *be the change* by allowing our mutual life force to flow into keeping the conversation open.

We can't change anyone else, but we can change ourselves. We can turn our passion into that which brings the new into being rather than championing a single side.

We might also *be the change* by not taking

a side at all! That would certainly move us to freedom.

Most of all, we can remind ourselves in every moment that the prevailing irritating issues are pure reality creation. That in the long run, they are meaningless.

In the new paradigm all issues will be looked upon side-by-side and each of us will respond from the heart center rather than to the thoughts and opinions residing in our heads. We will do this to live in the prevailing finer frequency that is coming. Now is the time to begin practicing so that we will be ready.

Harness the Power of Solar Plexus Energy

One of the fastest ways to get roped into taking sides on an issue, or to find yourself in conflict with another person, is to "have" feelings, descend into them, be overwhelmed by them. This phenomenon happens almost automatically because we are too prone to react rather than act. Once we are "in" the feelings it is not easy to lift above them and they take over our behavior.

When the transformation occurs our relationship to feelings will be very different because we will learn that we have the power to create them and when we do that, feelings do not "have us."

Creating rather than having feelings is somehing we can begin to practice right now as we prepare for the grand shift that is coming.

The solar plexus, wherein the energy for feeling response initiates, is one of our power centers. Just as we can have jurisdiction over the mind and configure thoughts rather than have them emerge from past experience; we can do the same with the solar plexus.

To do this we must function consciously, of course, and we need to be attuned to the stirring in our midsection when we are in conversation, or confronting a problem, or listening to the news, etc. If we pay attention, we will begin to feel energy moving.

In that very moment, we have an opportunity to use the life force that is awakening and configure it into the feeling we want to express. If we function consciously, we can exert power over what we feel and how we bring it forth. If we do this, we will not be overrun by emotions, or trapped by them.

The process is the same as what we do when we choose how to express ourselves through the heart center. With our awareness heightened we choose to be alert to the frequency churning in the solar plexus and we "catch" the energy and shape it into a response. The response we make will be the highest and best we can bring into reality and that response will imprint those around us and make a difference in the moment.

A profound example of this occurred many years before I knew about creating feelings rather than having them. It was my wake-up call to taking charge of feeling-creation.

I received a letter from one of the most important people in my life who accused me of doing things that simply were not true and who shut down all further communication. I was astounded and descended so quickly into solar plexus despair that I was sobbing and devastated.

My husband arrived home and found me in a literal heap. He instantly jumped into his protective mode and said he was going to kill the letter writer. He was furious. His response was so strong that it jarred me right out of my weeping and into finding an instant alternative to his feelings and mine. I didn't know if he was serious, but I did know that I needed to create a different response immediately.

I breathed into my very sore solar plexus and sent calming energy to soothe the uproar. Then I lifted into my heart center and told Dick what I needed from him was love and that I would find my way through to dealing with this situation.

I had made such a swift shift that he too

calmed down and could be there for me.

I moved from woundedness, pain, overwhelm, and despair (all of which I had created unconsciously and as a reaction) to taking responsibility for my energy output and choosing to send love to the letter writer. I realized almost immediately that when people sever communication or say hurtful things, they cannot stop me from sending love energy to them.

In this situation I did that every day for five years. When finally a reconnection occurred, the person took responsibility for all of it, saying she didn't have the capacity to deal with all the love and caring she felt for me, and she had to leave the friendship.

Although we had wasted precious time, years, I never lost out on the love that I shared with her in the energy world. I could still give, and though I couldn't sense anything coming back, it didn't matter. I was being the change. I continued to love. It was good.

Live in the Now Moment

Take a breath. Be here, right here. Be here, right now. This sounds very easy but if you try it, you might discover that your mind is already jumping to the next minute, to later today, to chores you must accomplish, etc. Being here right now and staying is a challenge. People practice this in meditation and whole techniques have been developed to facilitate this.

The phenomenon of living in the now-moment yields many benefits. All our awareness is gathered and applied to right now. You can feel a swelling of life force in your whole self, a lifting, a complete readiness, and a stirring in the crown chakra.

On a practical level, living in the now-moment means you are whole. Your attention is undivided. You are filled with a sense of power. Nothing is in your way, or behind you. You are present and there is complete silence in the whole of your field.

Imagine greeting every moment this way. There is nothing else. There is only now. Every step you take, every action, every word you say emerges from what is transpiring right now. It is like stepping forward into the pulse of life, into what is ready to emerge. You don't have to do anything; simply meet what is right in front of you.

I am describing a panacea. Most of us can't live this way all the time. We are lucky if we can touch it now and then. The more we practice, the better we will get.

We can at least begin by holding the concept that life is a never-ending series of now-moments. There is nothing else but now. If we remember this concept, all worry will disappear, all conjecture, all expectations. In effect, all the mental clutter in our lives will fall away.

Look for the Wisdom in Each Happening and Apply It to Self

Life will take on deeper meaning when we shift to greatness. We will lift out of mundane living, cliché and meaningless conversation, and moments passed unconsciously. We will no longer go on drift for long periods of time. Each moment will be filled with meaning and lead to creative acts. This will require that each of us breathes more deeply. That we draw in more energy consciously, that we think less and be and do and feel more.

Moments will be more important, more enlivened, and each will convey wisdom to us because wisdom is embedded in all life expressions. We will find ourselves asking more often when something happens, what does this mean? We will want to know. These moments will become teaching experiences.

One such experience for me occurred when I was 16. My boyfriend gave me a camera. I had never had one and knew nothing about photography. Because there was little to photograph in my neighborhood, I went to the Brooklyn Botanical Gardens to shoot pictures of flowers. I never suspected that I would discover a whole new side to life. I felt the flowers inside me, their texture and color. They pulsed with life. When the photos were developed, I saw that I had captured that life. The flowers in my photos were so rich, so alive it was as if I could touch them on the photo paper and feel their texture.

The wisdom that spoke to me in this experience was that seeing with the inner self, through the inner eye, far surpasses our physical vision. I never had any idea about that.

Not long after that, I began taking pictures of my friends. When they and I looked at the photographs we both agreed that I had seen into their soul and had captured that essence in my photos. This gift has greatly expanded over the last half century. Never having had a photography lesson, I could merge with what I was shooting and reproduce the inner life of it in the outer photo.

In my late teens I knew nothing of souls or inner life or essences. And yet, in that one initial moment in those gardens in Brooklyn I discovered a whole new world. It taught me that there was a wealth of untapped inner self that awaited my attention and awakening.

It is no wonder that my breakthrough to cosmic consciousness came while looking into a flower in Big Sur, CA thirteen years later. And it is no wonder that when I am fully present in each moment, I feel my profound connectedness with all that is.

Once we identify the wisdom or the learning, we will take it to the next step. This would mean applying that wisdom to self, to our ongoing lives. When I am functioning consciously and setting the intention to connect on a deep level, I don't just relate to others when we converse, I look into their souls and infuse myself with the beauty of their being. They feel seen, heard, and known as a result.

Each such applied learning will become part of our expanding selves, and our growth will escalate. Growth and consciousness will expand exponentially in ourselves and in others around us.

This in turn will expand even further as multiples of people do the same. This is what greatness will look like: human beings committed to inner growth, to embodying love, to expanding beyond previous limitations, to living in finer frequencies, to being points of light, to opening to the Divine.

From the point of view of my character self, my current personality, the above sounds exhausting, if not impossible. I like growing. I appreciate finding and applying wisdom. I am already a force of love and light. But doing it all the time? Becoming what seems like a consciousness giant who never ceases to touch and apply wisdom? Seems like a bit much.

And indeed, it is, in our current frequency realm. But the more is where we are heading. It is coming faster than we think.

Open to Oneness

Remind yourself every day that you are part of the larger whole, that you are a contributing cell in the One Creative Being and that your thoughts, feelings, and actions matter because they imprint the entire world in which we live.

We are One and yet each of us is unique, all of us contributing to the reality that emerges. Knowing that we are One enables us to expand our life experience as we are enriched by the grand variety of human expressions.

I like to imagine the One that we are, taking in a breath of life and exhaling it into creativity that lifts all of us into our emerging potential, into excellence, into the greater that awaits us.

Oneness, one cell in the body of the whole consciously joining with all other cells to enhance life.

Recently Mari and I sat in an audience of over a thousand people listening to Beethoven's 3rd piano concert played by the Scottsdale Philharmonic Orchestra. The air conditioning came on and caused Mari to begin coughing. She reached for her jacket and struggled to don it from a sitting position. I leaned over to help her pull it down in the back. Suddenly, there were four other hands and arms joining my two. I didn't see the people to whom these helping hands belonged, but I was instantly aware that there were now two hands in front (Mari's) and six hands in back, all enabling the adjustment of the jacket. Eight hands in the effort. Four people, all One. It was a remarkable moment.

The experience confirmed for me the power that exists in our acknowledgment that we are One Being creating a reality together. When we do this consciously, what we bring into being supports and lifts the Whole.

In Summary

The Universe is churning up its influence on humanity and on Planet Earth. Human divisiveness and warring have reached intolerable levels. Earth itself is under such threat from destructive human behavior that it cannot wait for humanity to reset its moral compass. The process is in motion and each of us is being called to prepare to live in greater intensity of Light and in the presence of higher realms.

Preparation is not only important so that we can make the shift, but also because it enables us to be active participants in the emergence of the transformation. By lifting ourselves beyond settling for "good," we commence living in the finer frequency even before it is a fact. If the cosmic transformation does not occur during our lifetime, our own transition into greatness and light allows us to live in the "new" even before it becomes a reality!

When we listen within and yield to what is wanted of us, we are raised from the good to the profound. We don't need to mentally comprehend the new that emerges for us. We need only to live it and thus discover the more of which we are capable.

In 1970 and since then, the focus of the Love Principle *Be the Change* was on becoming an alternative to what was troubling and on moving beyond seeking to change others.

Just as this book was about to go to press, I saw a deeper application, one that relates to preparation for the transformation: *Be the change that is coming!*

Become One with all that is. Expand from personal to Universal love expression. Move beyond competition to the fruitfulness of cooperation. Elevate your beliefs to unquestionable knowing. Let conflict dissolve and experience the power of co-existence. Fill your life with purpose and conscious direction. Become a vehicle of unconditional love. Banish fear and chose awe. Turn toward the Divine. Embody the light. Live in finer frequency.

This is what is ahead of us, and we can live it now.

Be the change that is coming.

****

It is as if we are all seated in a silent, darkened theatre awaiting a concert of the music of the spheres. The conductor's baton is suspended in the air. This is the moment before the moment.

Made in the USA
Columbia, SC
26 October 2024